WALKING THROUGH GRIEF

FINDING HOPE AND HEALING IN THE PSALMS OF LAMENT

MARK MEDLEY

Published by hope*books
2217 Matthews Township Pkwy
Suite D302
Matthews, NC 28105
www.hopebooks.com

hope*books is a division of hope*media Network

Printed in the United States of America

Image by rawpixel.com on Freepik

First paperback edition.
Paperback ISBN: 979-8-89185-000-2
Hardcover ISBN: 979-8-89185-014-9
ebook ISBN: 979-8-89185-001-9
Library of Congress Number: 2023915515

hb
hope*books
hopebooks.com
Because the world needs your hope-filled words now more than ever.

To My Melissa

TABLE OF CONTENTS

CHAPTER ONE

The Broken

How long, O Lord? Will you forget me forever?
How long will you hide your face from me?
How long must I take counsel in my soul
and have sorrow in my heart all day?
How long shall my enemy be exalted over me?
—Psalms 13:1–2

In our thirty-third year of marriage, my kind and beautiful wife Melissa died of pancreatic cancer. The news hit like an earthquake, the disease spread like a flood, and my family and I were left in what felt like the wake of a tornado. Though she was a healthy, beaming, brimming-with-love wife, mother, and friend, it was less than six months from diagnosis to death.

No words. Only cries…confusion…questions. How could this happen to such a good and godly person? Why should she suffer from such a terrible disease? What do

I do now? I don't know how to be a widower, a single parent, or a single grandparent. I'm not even sure who I am now without her. Or what I need to do. Or what needs to be done for this aching heart of mine. What do I do with the dreams we dreamt together?

These questions roll like thunder through the hollow of a hurting heart. On my grieving journey, some of these questions have been answered and some have not. But there are a few things I have come to understand. I have learned that having God near is better than knowing why. I have learned that both kindness and grief can take your breath away. And yet, knowing these things doesn't remove the pain. Something *must* be done with this pain.

Broken hearts are the fruit of a broken world. There must be an outlet for these emotions or else they fester and infect. Grief, I have found, can be its own form of cancer, eating away at hope, peace, and sleep—so we can't ignore our feelings. But, negative expressions of these feelings can be even more destructive, rippling the effects of the pain we feel outward to those around us. There has to be a positive way to deal with the negative in our world. And there is. It's called the gift of *lament*.

The Bible has an entire category of literature dedicated to dealing with our emotions. Laments are found often in the words of the prophets but mostly in the book of Psalms. Of the one hundred and fifty songs included in the Psalter, at least one-third can be categorized as laments. So what is a lament? It is a passionate cry of pain to God that ends in hope. It is also a pathway by which we process the hurt of our hearts in a healthy way. It is a way to deal with emotional toxins in a nontoxic way.

The Bible gives sometimes beautiful, sometimes furious, and sometimes desperate expressions to the feelings of sorrow, fear, and pain that we all feel at times. When we don't have the words, the Psalms give us something real and honest to pray. They are not only a comfort but they are also a guide.

Lamenting Psalms are written by a variety of authors, living at different times and experiencing unique problems—but amazingly, they almost always use a similar pattern in dealing with their pain. This pattern has helped me process my own loss. I think it will help you, too.

This book is my personal story of how God is guiding me through my grief. I have found that even in the midst of my pain there is a pathway to hope. As I shared my grief journey and what God was showing me through the lamenting psalms, my friends from many parts of the world told me, "You should write a book about what you have learned." I wanted to punch them.

Of course, I never would have done that, but it is impossible for me to tell you how much the thought of writing a book on grief repulsed me. How do you write about what is crushing your heart and pulling you into pieces? And besides, simple steps to grief resolution are almost an insult to those who are in the throes of their loss. My ache was not academic. It was intensely emotional, shaking me to my bones. Grief is as unique as your own soul and circumstance. Your journey of pain is deeply personal and a personal God will guide you through.

Write a book? It was impossible for me to think about chronicling my grief process. I couldn't even wrap my mind around *wrapping my mind around* what I was experiencing. No, I would never write a book about grief.

Then I took a bike ride on a brilliantly sunny afternoon by the river and through the ridges of my beautiful native East Tennessee. By the end of that ride, my Father had shown me a way that writing a book to help others through this valley of grief might be possible. If I wrote about this verdant valley around me and the mountains that surround it—the struggle and the beauty of my homeland—and wrote about my and Melissa's families along with others who settled here, if I used it to parallel our grief journey and the biblical process of lament, then maybe...just maybe.

The beauty of East Tennessee is not merel renowned natural beauty. It is the beauty of the people, it is the beauty of the struggle. And yes, I have found that there is beauty in struggle, for there is kindness and presence and strength and deep roots in Christ there. The mountains and foothills of the Smokies hold something special. They have been a safety and solace for me all my days. My friend Rick summed it up when he said:

> *When we see Mount Rainier or Pike's Peak or El Capitan, we use words like majestic, awesome, imposing, breathtaking—manifestations of God's awe. But these southern mountains are God's listeners. They cover, they comfort, they encourage. And they whisper to us how well-loved we are.*

Yes, I have these mountains and this long valley to listen and comfort me. They were the soundtrack of my and Melissa's lives together—a continuous thread through the tapestry of our marriage. But much more than these, in my devastation I've found that I have a Father who weeps with me, a Man of Sorrows who is acquainted with grief, and a Comforter inside who tenderly guides me.

In this book, I want to tell my story of love and loss and love still. I want to tell the struggled story of our own families here in this Tennessee Valley. I want to tie it together with the pathway to hope and healing God shows us in the lamenting Psalms. Surely you could replace my locale for yours and tell the stories of your cherished place—wherever home is, these kinds of deep connections are bound to be. This is simply my story, set in my beloved homeland.

The Ride

As I was riding my bike through that valley, along the riverbank, and through the surrounding ridges that day, another valley flashed into my mind: the valley of weeping spoken of in Psalm 84. Scholars say this may be a literal place, but it is certainly a symbol for all kinds of hurt we endure on our journey through a broken world. The psalmist sings to the Lord, whose presence he longs for:

> *Blessed are those whose strength is in you,*
> *in whose heart are the highways to Zion.*
> *As they go through the Valley of Baca [weeping]*
> *they make it a place of springs;*
> *the early rain also covers it with pools.*
> *They go from strength to strength;*
> *each one appears before God in Zion.*
> *—Psalms 84:5–7*

Baca is the valley of tears. It is wherever we experience brokenness. Tears of deep, wrenching sorrow; tears of loss and loneliness; tears of helplessness and humiliation; tears of disappointment, depression, and repentance. These are the tears of the vulnerable and abandoned; tears of shame and regret. They are the overflow of a heart journeying through pain. For me, it was the loss of my treasure, Melissa. But grief is not relegated to losing a loved one to death—it can be the loss of a marriage, a job, or a dream. It can be an estranged relationship. We mourn when our expectations aren't met or when sickness comes and stays. We cry out when our loved ones suffer. There are ten thousand weepings in a wounded world, but lament is the prescription for them all.

Psalm 84 is about people who long for the presence of their God. They understand this relationship is a journey and this highway includes dark places...valleys of weeping. Yet these are not places of despair only. They are moments to know the One we love more deeply. These tears of grief can become wells of water springing up and strengthening your soul.

This is a book about living in the tensions of heartbreak and hope. Ultimately, it is a book about kindness, for on my journey through my own Baca, God's kindness has covered and carried me at every turn. Kindness and hope are what God offers us in our dark places. I am walking through this valley, and I have a message for you: A wounded world and a faithful Father can live together. This is my story…this is my song.

But before I begin, I have to tell you another story.

Eighteen months after Melissa died, I was traveling in Europe training pastors and church leaders. One day I was sitting in a restaurant at the Museum of the History of Polish Jews in Warsaw, Poland. The restaurant serves Jewish food—Kosher and crazy delicious—and I sat at a table with my friends and our culinary delights. Suddenly, the pastor's wife looked up and remarked, "You know what's unusual about Jewish food? They can take things that are bitter and put them with things that are sweet… and somehow it works."

We nodded in agreement, not wanting to stop chewing long enough to answer back. As I pondered her statement, I noticed the Jewish folk music playing over the intercom. It was up-tempo and celebratory, yet it was in a minor key—a key that Western minds often associate with sadness or solemnity.

It dawned on me at that moment that Jewish people know a secret we in the West have yet to learn. Bitter and sweet can coexist. The minor key and joy can go together. We tend to think if we can separate ourselves from our pain—insulate ourselves from our troubles, buffer our suffering—we can live a better life. The problem is, it's not possible to do that on this earth. Where we live, brokenness happens to all of us.

But grief and goodness can happen *at the same time*. This is the message in nearly every one of the lamenting Psalms. This is also the message I have for you. The season since Melissa's illness and death has been brutal. But the kindness and presence of God have been beautiful. Brutal but beautiful: it has been *brutiful*. *Brutiful* is the word that best expresses my experience because heartache and hope can live together, in the same heart, at the same time.

In my loss, I can walk with Jesus *and* with grief at the same time—and the Holy Spirit will guide us on this journey down a roadway called lament. The traditional stages of grief we may be familiar with (denial, anger, bargaining, depression, acceptance) can make grief seem like a linear process: as if walking through these steps will result in healing. Those of us who have grieved deeply understand that our loss comes to us again and again, often when we least expect it and in ways that aren't always rational.

This linear thinking is more of a Western mindset. It's a convenient way to think about grief, but it is not the full truth of it. In the lamenting Psalms of the Bible, we see something different—a way to deal with the cyclical nature of grief, those recurring pangs of loss that come from triggered memories or that simply come from out of nowhere.

In searching God's word for a healthy way to deal with my grief, I have noticed a pattern that is present in nearly every one of the lamenting Psalms, as well as many passages in the prophets. I was greatly helped in my understanding of Psalms of Lament by Mark Vroegop's *Dark Clouds, Deep Mercy*.[1] It's not a simple step-by-step process, for grief is complicated. There is no precise order, for in pain we do not think or react systematically. But, there *are* steps that appear in most lamenting psalms. Though there are many variations, it looks something like this:

- **The Broken:** We feel, deeply and personally, the painful effects of living in this wounded world.
- **The Gap:** We see the wide space between the way we know things should be and the way things are.
- **The Turn:** We allow our pain to press us into God, not pull us away.
- **The Cry:** We bare our honest emotions, fears, and anger openly to God.
- **The Reveal:** God opens our eyes to a deeper understanding of who He is and what He has done.
- **The Wait:** From this revelation, we recognize and surrender to His work in us, and faith rises within us.

1 Mark Vroegop, *Dark Clouds, Deep Mercy: Discovering the Grace of Lament* (Wheaton: Crossway, 2019).

- **The Walk:** Our daily, practical, trusting response to God.
- **The Hope:** The beauty of the gospel promise applied to our pain.

The wise men of the ages have understood that valuable life lessons are learned in the midst of our pain. The "School of Sorrow" is not a physical place but a journey of learning. There are things we can never understand unless we see them through the eyes of suffering. Throughout the book, you will find inserts of *Wisdom from the School of Sorrow*. These are collections of wise insights I have compiled from fellow grievers who share their experiences of walking through loss in various forms. They help us answer some of the most common questions concerning the grieving process. You will see their wisdom and their names at the end of each chapter.

There are also many helpful books that deal with the physical, psychological, and practical issues of grief.[2] I am not a doctor or psychiatrist. I am a pastor, a teacher, and a widower; so, this book will focus on my understanding and experience of the pathway to healthy grieving that God gives us in the Psalms.

---

2 See Notes at the end of the book for the complete list of books referenced that deal with the physical, psychological, and practical issues of grief.

Our Story

The death of a loved one is an incalculable loss. This is partly because of the immeasurable value of the image of God in every human. But in a more intimate way, it is because of what that person was to us. We who know them best naturally grieve the loss deeper. Who Melissa was and what we had together is a testimony to the goodness of God. It is also the reason for the pain we now know because of her loss.

God brought both Melissa and me out of difficult backgrounds: she from a dysfunctional and abusive family and me from a life of drugs and immoral relationships. We both knew Jesus for many years before we knew each other, and He had changed us from the inside out. She was the answer to my prayer for a good and godly wife. We grew close as friends and prayer partners before we realized He might have given us each other as marriage partners. From the beginning, there was a purity in our relationship that I had not known before.

After two years of marriage, the children came like a tide. Melissa bore four in less than three years—Katie, Emily and Allison (identical twin girls), and Zac. We scurried much and slept little during those years, me working as a pastor and musician (and other jobs as needed) and Melissa laboring equally hard at home. We took our parenting seriously and did it together, homeschooling all four children through twelve years of school.

We also learned that if we were not serious about keeping our marriage a priority, it would be swallowed up by the urgent needs of day-to-day life. So we were fiercely focused, hewing out time for each other with weekly dates and periodic trips away (usually to our beloved mountains). And as the kids grew, married, and left the house, we were still in love with each other. We had the best marriage I knew. And we had many dreams of what our future together might look like.

I do not write these things to boast but to give glory to God and to let you know why I call Melissa my treasure. Of course, not everything was easy. We were painfully aware of our own faults and selfishness. The normal conflicts of marriage and of parenting (four infants, four toddlers, four "tween-agers," and four teens in succession) were part of our everyday lives. Money problems, conflicts with extended families, health concerns, all of life's curveballs—we swung at them all.

Melissa graciously bore the burden of a pastor's wife—one of the most unsung and heroic jobs on earth. She supported me in my calling to travel and train church leaders worldwide, often joining me to speak on building healthy families. She invested time and money in helping our children in their marriages and parenting.

She often sat over coffee or tea, helping other young women grow in their character, their knowledge of God, and their practical life skills. She was a kind, pleasant, and beautiful person and a deeply devoted friend.

This is why my loss is incalculable. This is why I need to know what to do with this grief and how to navigate this new world. This is why I need the gift of lament.

Lament Is a Gift

I have found lament to be a *holy space*—a place of honesty and revelation. It is a journey toward understanding, even when we don't understand, like the hovering of the Spirit at creation:

In the beginning, God created the
heavens and the earth.
The earth was without form and void, and
darkness was over the face of the deep.
And the Spirit of God was hovering
over the face of the waters.
—Genesis 1:1–2

In the same way, God is present and His Spirit hovers over us in our grief, turning chaos into order, speaking light, and creating something that will shout his glory.

Lament is also an *active space*—like the overshadowing of the Spirit upon Mary:

"And the angel answered her, 'The Holy Spirit will come upon you, and the power of the Most High will overshadow you; therefore the child to be born will be called holy—the Son of God'" —Luke 1:35

Similarly, God is at work in our grieving, forming the character and image of his Son in us, even in our lowest place. What we need most in our grief is Jesus, and He is what we find in the darkness over and over again. I am slowly coming to see my grief as a beautiful way to honor Melissa and the love we had. It is a natural extension and a raw and true expression of my love for her. Melissa is worth the pain I am feeling, but she is also worth celebrating. Lament helps me do both.

A Royal Example

In Psalm 13, King David pours out his pain before the Lord. He travels each footstep of the journey of lament: He turns, cries, sees, waits, walks... and in the end, He hopes in the kindness that covers and carries Him.

David knew that the God of the covenant had told his suffering people, "Every place that the sole of your foot will tread upon I have given you, just as I promised Moses" (Josh. 1:3). The very imprint of their feet in the soil of their Valley of Baca was a signature on the deed to the land. In the same way, we take new ground. We inherit new places in God as we walk our journey of lament. The goal is not merely getting past our emotional pain. The true goal is walking together with the One whose love and presence are healing to our spirit, soul, and body.

I hope to offer you a safe place. A feeling of home, nestled in the beauty of God's creation. The safety of empathy from a fellow traveler through this valley of weeping. And most of all, the safe words of the Psalms that have been the balm to generations of God's people in this valley of tears.

Wisdom from the School of Sorrow

How Can I Open Up When I'm Hurting?

I am in the process of receiving physical therapy for a torn Achilles tendon. Part of the healing process is allowing the physical therapist to apply significant pressure in order to help loosen the scar formation. Needless to say, it hurts!

I grit my teeth and endure the treatment because this temporary pain will actually be the pathway to health. Why would I want someone to touch an area that is already hurting? If I don't believe my physical therapist has my best interests at heart, I will not let my guard down and let them "hurt" me.

How much more does this analogy apply to the emotional and spiritual aspects of our lives? I can assume a posture of self-protection and withdraw inside to the perceived safety of my mind. But I have to choose to open myself up if I want to receive healing. I believe transparency can open up an avenue for light to begin to enter darkened places. Unconditional love provides the safety to risk emotional exposure. (Roger V.)

CHAPTER TWO

The Gap

Behold, these are the wicked;
always at ease, they increase in riches.
All in vain have I kept my heart clean
and washed my hands in innocence.
For all the day long I have been stricken
and rebuked every morning.
—Psalms 73:12–14

Rugged and rumpled, like a carpet crumpled over the fields and rivers of Appalachia, these mountains of mine roll as far as you care to look in either direction. Ridges piled upon one another as if striving to be the first to touch the azure blue, their slopes giving way to the broad river basins in between. The foothills roll like gentle waves down to the banks of the river that carved this valley ages ago.

This is my home. I love to bike and hike among the hundreds of miles of trails in and around the Great

Smoky Mountains National Park. It's the most visited park in the United States National Park system; once you come here, you know why. Just walk beside a mountain stream, trace it till you see a waterfall, climb to the top of a ridge, and try your best to breathe in the vista. You can watch it all your life and never take it in. I know. And you can walk a trail from here to nearly Canada if you want.

But I live in the valley—really, nestled among the ridge-and-valley folds of the greater East Tennessee Valley. Within a few miles of my house, you'll find Brushy Valley, Bull Run Valley, Raccoon Valley, and Wolf Valley, with ridge lines between them all. Not rugged, jutted ridges but a rolling range of mountains softened by the nap of deciduous and conifer trees. Not far from these ridges, the gentle roll of the hills will lull you into the calm before you know it, with farmhouses and barns and silos stretching to the sky, filled with the fruit of the labor of unsung heroes who work this land for the rest of us.

This land was as welcoming to its first inhabitants as it is to us today. But don't let the gentle beauty fool you. The Cumberland Mountains are a solid, impregnable wall of rock that kept all things east from getting to the west for hundreds of years.

Except for the gap: Cumberland Gap. It is there, where Virginia, Kentucky, and Tennessee kiss, that buffalo and elk first passed through, then the Cherokee and Shawnee Indians, and then European hunters and scouts and settlers came through the mountains.

In 1775, Daniel Boone was hired to blaze a trail through The Gap and over land purchased from the Cherokee Indians. It was nothing more than a rough and stony path, barely wide enough for a single wagon, but it was the most passable way through the mountains. By way of this "Wilderness Road," hundreds of thousands of people passed into the territories of Kentucky, Tennessee, and farther west in the early years of our nation. Through much danger, with much loss, they crossed over and into a fresh start filled with freedom and promise.

The Gap, you see, was a threshold—a liminal space. It was that in-between place where you aren't where you were, but you aren't yet where you're going to be. It was the tension and uncertainty of letting go of what was in order to embrace what will be. No one likes these in-between places, right?

I have found that the grief process is also a gap; a threshold. It feels like you are stuck in the middle. As much as you might like to move on, you realize something is going on inside—a sometimes furious and sometimes gentle gestation—but you can't hurry the process. Grief takes as long as it takes. And the uncomfortable thing is that we are not in control of it.

This liminal space brings us face-to-face with things we didn't realize were inside us. It tests everything we thought was true. It makes us question our identity and our core beliefs. It causes us to rearrange the price tags of all things in our lives. It forces us to let go of the control we thought we held and, instead, trust something higher than ourselves. Here at the threshold, everything changes. But the beauty is that our Bridegroom will carry us over this threshold.

Our Dark Valley

Biking through these ridges, through sunshine and tree-tunneled paths, the muscles burn in my legs like the questions burn in my soul. The beauty of the valley before me contrasts with the fear and uncertainty of the Valley of Baca inside me. The gap in Psalm 84 is a valley of weeping, and this gap appears in all of the lamenting Psalms in one form or another. It is the chasm created when what we believe and what we are experiencing clash—and sometimes crash. We feel the tension, body, and soul: twisting, testing, wresting, and forming Christ within us, even in the midst of our dark valley.

When we found out Melissa had pancreatic cancer, it was already stage four and had metastasized to her liver. It was a rare and aggressive type, and we immediately went to work doing everything we knew to do. We employed every treatment available: traditional, nontraditional, nutritional, homeopathic, pharmaceutical, psychological, and spiritual. Besides local treatment, we traveled to two internationally acclaimed cancer hospitals for treatment. We had strong-faithed believers praying on five continents. We were unshakable in our belief that God could heal her physical body and we contended for that.

The doctors told us this type of cancer grows so fast they don't know much about it since there is never enough time to study it effectively. It is usually not detected until the late stages, and if left untreated, life expectancy is one month; with treatment, two months. But Melissa was a fighter. She loved her family and wanted to live. She hung on for six long and grueling months. She did everything she was asked and did it well. She kept a quiet and kind heart, even through all the pain, until her last conscious moments.

Those last moments were a tribute to Melissa's life. The family encircled her bed, a ring of love that rang out with songs from broken voices and eyes swollen with tears. We had worshipped together in many ways throughout the years, and now, this one last time with her (on earth), a song arose. That sterile smell of hospital room, those beeping monitors, the IV dripping pain meds—yet through that mess of brokenness, the beautiful hope of a song of praise sung over her by those she had loved most in life. *Brutiful.*

My darling girl passed away, at 2:30 a.m. on Yom Kippur, the Jewish Day of Atonement. The kids and I sat in silence for a while, talked a little—there is little to say in a moment like that—then left the hospital. The September chill wrapped around me as I walked through the darkness to the car. The deserted streets reminded me that I was alone now in a way I had never planned for. I'm sure I've never heard silence so deafening as I did that night lying in bed, trying to sleep.

The morning broke, a glorious East Tennessee autumn day; there was such beauty all around yet such horrible pain inside. What happens now? What do you do when the one God gave you to complete you is gone? The two were made one, and now one is no more. Am I half a person?

I stood on the back deck of our house, facing the forest of trees already turning their fall colors. Soft sunlight filtered through the branches. The cardinals were still singing their lilting melodies. The air was clear, laced with a gentle scent from the flowers I had bought the day before. We were planning to bring Melissa home from the hospital for hospice care, and I had spruced up the deck area, knowing that she could sit in her recliner and look out the double French doors to see some beauty. Along with the flowers, I had stopped to buy her some looser pants—her pants were pressing against the tumors and causing pain. I had felt so desperately helpless that in her time of greatest need, all I could do was buy her flowers and pants. But we love however we can.

I remembered how the night before my daughter Katie sat with Melissa, and I came home to prepare the flowers and the medical equipment she would need when she was discharged from the hospital. I received the call that she had taken a turn for the worse and I should come quickly and call the family in. I remembered when I walked out of the house, the thought pierced me—I may never walk back into this house with the love of my life.

The drive, the whirlwind of confusing thoughts, the surreal reality we found ourselves in. And then I recalled, as I walked into the hospital, the voice of my Lord, inaudible, but loud and clear inside me: "I know what I am doing."

All of these thoughts ran like a river through my mind as I stood on that deck. A gentle breeze eased me somehow. Was it the wind or the Spirit? I thought of David when he found out his son had died after so many prayers and tears. He rose, washed, and worshiped. I remembered the kindness of God to us throughout the entire process, so many stories I could tell of His presence with us, His provision for us, and His people standing beside us. Goodness and grief at once amalgamated and inseparable.

I know who my Father is. I know He is kind, for I have experienced decades of His forgiveness and many-layered love. He has proven himself trustworthy to me. I don't see His kindness in my wife's death, but I believe it. *This is the Gap*. This tension, this liminal space of grief, is in nearly every lamenting psalm. Lament is a gift to us because it shows us a pathway from pain to promise and guides us to a place of hope. The kindness of God waits at every turn in the sorrowful songs of scripture.

What also appears in the lamenting Psalms are enemies. There are many different types of enemies, but they are ever-present in these heart hymns to God. I have learned that I must name my enemies in order to fight them. So it is important to probe our pain to learn exactly what we are feeling.

Is it a devastating loss that is punching a hole in your heart?

Is fear paralyzing you and mocking your future?

Is desperation forcing you to the limit of your resources?

Is hopelessness persuading you that nothing will ever change?

Is anger at injustice pushing you to the breaking point?

Is sin the problem—do you need to repent?

Whatever the enemy, the psalmist was self-aware enough to call it out and cry it out to God. In the months after Melissa died, I wasn't exactly sure what my enemies were. Grief is a funnel cloud that sucks you up and takes you, twisting and tumbling, to an unfamiliar place. It confuses your bearings. You don't know what to do because you don't know where you are, and you're not sure what is ahead of you. I needed space to encounter God's grace.

Listening in the Gap

It is important to get quiet and listen while in the Gap because grief is the greatest teacher. The wise men of the ages have understood that there are valuable life lessons to be learned in the School of Sorrow. Solomon may have never penned more true—nor more confusing—words than he did in Ecclesiastes:

> *It is better to go to the house of mourning than to go to the house of feasting, for this is the end of all mankind, and the living will lay it to heart.*
> *Sorrow is better than laughter, for by sadness of face the heart is made glad.*
> *The heart of the wise is in the house of mourning, but the heart of fools is in the house of mirth.*
> —Ecclesiastes 7:2–4

Grief is a great teacher mostly because it is a great revealer. It shows us parts of ourselves that can be uncomfortable but which we need to face honestly. It reveals where we have put our trust, the places to which we have turned for safety, security, identity, and provision. It reveals which friends are true friends. It reveals wisdom about the brevity of life and what things are most important. Most of all, it reveals the heart, the works, and the ways of the Living God. The God who stoops down and weeps over us and lifts us up.

Everyone is different when it comes to how they face their grief. We don't have to deal with it the same way others do, but we do have to deal with it. I realized I couldn't let grief settle or it would fester and spread its poison. I had to name my enemies and find my way of facing them.

Each of us has different ways of adapting to change. My Melissa had her own method of getting into a swimming pool. She would dip her toes in and check the temperature. Then came the entire foot and, in a few minutes, above the ankle. Then, after a while, above the knee. She just needed some time to adjust her body. But to me that is torture! The only way for me to get in is to dive right into the deep end, feel the shock, and get it over with.

Some people need to ease their way into grieving. They have to linger in safe places, take no big risks, and make no major decisions. No doubt, there is wisdom in this approach. But others feel the need to jump right in, invite the scalpel, and give full liberty to the surgeon—right now.

I am not telling you this is the way you should process your grief. I just want to tell you how I was led on this journey and what I found in the process. The right way is the way that works for you. For me, I had to go for it—travel to places Melissa and I used to go, face it, feel it, grieve it, and let Jesus speak to it. But there were things to tend to first.

Those first days after a loved one's passing often feel numb. We can tend to shift our feelings into neutral as much as possible and just do the next thing required of us. It was different for my family. The week after Melissa died, our entire family came down with COVID-19—all four of our children, their spouses, and the grandchildren were out of commission. Later that week, my oldest daughter gave birth to a son after thirty hours of labor and a C-section, while she herself had COVID-19 and her husband was stuck in Africa. No one in the family could be with her because we were infected with the virus. It was not an easy time for any of us.

Two weeks later, after everyone had recovered, we had Melissa's memorial service. The church was packed. She would have loved to have seen everyone who came, but she would have been uncomfortable being the center of attention.

The kids and I worked together to make the service as "Melissa-like" as we could. Blended aromas of cardamom, cinnamon, clove, and ginger, all laced with vanilla—a smell she would have loved—wafted through the sanctuary from essential oil diffusers situated in strategic areas. Serving tables were laid out with cups of Earl Grey tea and biscotti for those who were waiting in the receiving line. In every direction, there were flower displays and a waterfall fountain graced the platform. A slideshow of her greatest pics streamed on the screen, and the place was alive with people talking. The kids wrote and recorded a song in her honor. I pre-recorded an instrumental song that I had written for her before we were married called "My Melissa."

Those who spoke at the service had such deep and meaningful memories of their friend. We laughed together; we wept together; it was *brutiful.* It was the Gap—wide and clear—between the tragedy of what we lost and the beauty of what God gave us. He has been good to us. But oh God, how this hurts. God, what we have lost. Where is the good here?

The week after her memorial service I spent some time individually with each of my children. The team of pastors I served with was generous enough to extend my sabbatical for one more month, and I was off on a journey through several states, visiting places Melissa and I loved to go together. I spent a day at the very spot I proposed to her more than thirty-three years before—hallowed ground to me because it was there she said yes and forever changed my life. I visited bed-and-breakfasts, small tourist towns, mountain parkways, and beaches, all the places she loved to go.

This might seem like a frightful or even harmful way to mourn. Some people would never do it this way, I know. But it has been right for me. I needed to jump full into the pool—to face the hurtful things, to feel them fully, to mourn them, to cry out to God, and to listen for His perspective. This is the way it works best for me. Your Shepherd will lead you in your own way.

My Process (Not Necessarily Yours)

I felt compelled toward three steps of grieving during this sabbatical. First, to process the events of the last six months of Melissa's life. This was important because while we were experiencing the trauma and treatments, we were just doing the next thing on the list and trying to make everything as comfortable as possible for her. It is impossible to really process it while you are going through it. During this first step, I was recalling Melissa's fight, reviewing personal journals—both hers and mine—listening to recordings of conversations with medical professionals, and remembering hospital stints and times of care at home.

I found this to be one of the most difficult parts of my entire grieving process. Deep sorrow came from the fact that, as much as I wanted to and as much as I tried to, I felt I could never give Melissa all that she needed. Every grimace, every groan of pain was like a shot through my own soul. I felt so tragically powerless to give her what she needed.

Sometimes grief is a dull ache. Sometimes you almost forget about your loss for a while, distracted by daily life. But other times the tidal wave of grief is so visceral it doubles you over. What a stomach virus does to your body—there is no stopping the vomiting—this gush of grief does to your emotions. You can't do anything to stop the crying; you just have to let it run its course. But it is important to know that, just as vomiting is a way of getting rid of harmful substances in your body, crying is a healthy way your body responds to negative emotions. It is a path toward healing, not a weakness.

Yet there was something else going on in my processing. All the while, I was sensitive to the hovering of the Spirit over me and my grief-ladened soul. I could sense Jesus with his arms outstretched and saying (even to me, even there in my pain), "Come to me… I will give you rest" (Matt. 11:28).

What load was I bringing to Jesus? The weight of an unfathomable loss, of unanswered questions, of mental and physical exhaustion, and of unsureness about the future. Yet in the Gap, my eyes were opened to realize the extreme kindness God showed us through this time. I will write more about this in later chapters.

The second part of the sabbatical was looking back and chronicling the thirty-five years that Melissa and I knew each other. From the first time we met, through our courtship and proposal, and to the wedding, honeymoon, and setting up house. I recalled her giving birth to our four children and every season of raising them together. I remembered the jobs, serving the church together, the very difficult times, and the times of abundant blessings. There were two things I saw that brought healing—one expected and one unexpected. First, it was so glaringly obvious that God was faithful to us in every way throughout our marriage. His generous, guiding, grace-giving heart was in every memory.

But the second and most surprising thing he showed me was that we were faithful too. Carried by the grace and kindness of our Father to us, we were also loyal stewards of what came from His hand. We were faithful to Him, to each other, to our children, and to the church we served. We certainly didn't do everything right, and I would take many "re-dos" if it were possible, but one phrase kept showing up as I wrote out the account of our relationship: *We did it right, baby.* This is, in its own way, a source of healing.

The third step was about looking to the future. There are so many practical questions that must be answered. Where will I live? What financial decisions need to be addressed? How do I maintain relationships with my family and friends? The first tendency is to ask, "What am I supposed to *do* now?" But, I have found that more important than the "do" questions are the "be" questions. What is God specifically doing in me? What is he making me to be? How will I choose to live with this loss? What things do I know for sure? Where are the anchors in my life?

The Pathway in the Psalms

Along with these sabbatical steps, I also began another journey through the lamenting Psalms of the Bible. In those brutally honest expressions of God's suffering people, my Father graciously opened my eyes to a pathway of healthy grieving, and that is what I want to share with you in this book.

When we are grieving, we are in between in that most uncomfortable place, and we may be uncomfortable for a long time. But we can learn to be all right with being in process, for the process is changing us. It has taken me a while to get here, but I have come to view every pang of grief as the work of God forming in me a tiny, irregular piece of precious stone, polishing and placing it in just the right spot for the master mosaic He is creating that will reveal his glory.

I do believe He is at work. I can feel it, although I don't know what he is doing, and I don't even know what to pray for because I don't know exactly what I need. When we lose a loved one, there are so many things we've never faced before: those first holidays without her; learning to cook for one; doing the budget alone; paying the medical bills and dealing with doctors and insurance companies; and of course, everyday life and work and relationships don't stop. The challenges can seem overwhelming, and we can feel ill-equipped for the task.

The trail has shifted. But hasn't He proven Himself trustworthy all these years? Like those pioneers who trod across the Gap on the Wilderness Road that Daniel Boone blazed, I've never been this way before, but I have a personal trailblazer. One tempted in all points like me yet without sin. One who is acquainted with grief.

These emotions I feel are not enemies in themselves. I have them because I am made in the image of a God who lives and loves and, therefore, mourns. I shouldn't slough them off but pay attention to them, for God is speaking and working.

Psalm 73 is a classic "in-between" psalm, the cry of a person twisted by the tension of what is happening to him. Why do those who do not regard God prosper while I try to serve Him and suffer? We have likely all prayed a prayer like this and turned to God with the questions. I certainly did, and living with this kind of inner conflict is difficult.

But this hard place is a threshold for the psalmist. He arrives at an understandable, but wrong, conclusion. And then he finds he has too simplistic a view. He finds his answer when he turns to God in the sanctuary—it is there that his perspective is widened and wisdom comes. His hurtful place is a space of grace where God begins to show himself as a faithful and righteous judge. In the School of Sorrow, a fresh understanding of God appears.

God, you are near…you keep me near. You see me, you guide me, and one day you will receive me into glory. Your nearness is my strength.

The Gift of the Gap

The Gap gives us a chance to remember and honor the past. It allows us to press in to know Jesus more today. It offers us hope as we hear God's voice for the future. Celebration, intimacy, vision: all of these come to us through the gift of lament.

I have also found that a broken heart is an open heart—open to receive wisdom and the balm of healing from the Father, the solace of the Man of Sorrows, and comfort from the Comforter. Of course, a broken heart can also close in on itself and cut itself off from the very life, love, and healing it requires to keep beating. What makes the difference? Probably all the things we are uncomfortable with: surrender the admission that I don't know how to do this; faith to believe in goodness when I don't feel it. But we have a superpower in the midst of our grief. We have the ability to choose to remain connected and responsive to God.

In the lamenting Psalms, in the midst of pain and very real enemies, a very important first step toward healing happens. Lament is turning to God, even with our doubts, our anger, and our fears. But lament is not a lack of faith; it is the truest kind of faith, and it is a costly and precious cry of worship to God. Lament is always an effort to maintain a relationship.

My laments are all love songs—sung both to Melissa (for the loss of her) and to God (because I long to stay close to Him). And always, out of desperation and pain, the lamenter has a decision to make. Do I turn *to* God or *away* from God?

Wisdom from the School of Sorrow

How long does grief take?

Grief is tied to love. As long as we love the person, we will grieve the person—there is no time limit. Though grief doesn't end, it does change. Or more specifically, we change and view grief from a different perspective.

Grief is not a linear process with a beginning and ending but rather cyclical. It seems to ebb and flow like waves, some small and some huge. Its shape and intensity depend on the relationship you had with the person. Allow each step to happen in whatever order surfaces.

As Christians, we learn to grieve with hope and to be comforted by God's presence and promises. It seems to get easier the more you pay attention to the feelings, face them, and apply truth to them.

Quote:

There is no time limit to grief, and it varies from individual to individual. When one first loses a loved one, the physical and emotional pain and fog can be overwhelming due to the intensity. It gradually lessens as one assimilates the loss into one's life. However, it can ambush one again at any moment as the years pass and when it is least expected, triggered by anything. Traumatic grief often compounds the intensity and length of time before one can begin to feel a semblance of normalcy. For me, it took eighteen months before I could begin to even breathe deeply after the loss of our son. The pain of his loss is ever-present, though not in the forefront of my mind. Surviving grief is hard work and takes effort and determination to overcome the loss and to move forward. (Christine P.)

CHAPTER THREE

The Turn

With my voice I cry out to the Lord;
with my voice I plead for plead
for mercy to the Lord.
I pour out my complaint before him;
I tell my trouble before him.
—Psalms 142:1–2

My favorite bike path always demands of me a choice. To my left, the wider, more inviting way runs by the road—so I can get the exercise I need, have it over with, and get back home. This choice is quick and sterile, a good enough workout. In this direction, there are cars and concrete, but the other choice holds wonder. On this day I felt the need to take the path that pulls from me the most effort and delivers the most beauty.

So I set off, racing the roll of the river past the marsh where the cranes stand tall in the shallows—past the thicketed meadow, spotted yellow with coneflowers, and brown-eyed yellow heads dangling heavy on tall and lanky stems. Nectar-laden honeysuckle and pungent mosses blend and nibble at my nostrils. Then into the woods, the path leads me winding and climbing and pushing back against my resolve.

There is something in us all that wants to choose the path of least resistance. But there is also something further down—perhaps the voice of wisdom, or adventure, or just the need for more than we've had before—that calls out to us: *take the harder road*.

The way through The Gap was not an easy way for these pioneers. The Wilderness Road was fraught with peril, but the most difficult part of the entire journey may have been mustering the resolve to set out in the first place, given their past. They would be committing to the unknown—yet again. They would have to be rigid and resilient and depend upon themselves and very few of each other at first. Throughout the 1700s, my family and other settlers came to the New World from Germany, England, and Wales, but most who found their way to East Tennessee were Scots-Irish.

The Scots had struggled to gain a homeland for centuries when they were given land in Northern Ireland by King James (yes, of KJV fame) in the early 1600s. By most accounts, it was a consolation given just to be rid of them. But religious persecution, famines, and fatigue from fending off the harsh environment and invaders from outside made them look with a longing eye toward America. Now known as Scots-Irish, they pulled up their roots and their muddled identity and made the long, treacherous trip in rickety wooden ships across the Atlantic.

But the colonies were not to be their Promised Land. The entire eighteenth century saw the English, French, and Native Americans mired in combat throughout Appalachia. It was said a man could live from boyhood to old age and never know a time of peace.

The centuries-long struggle to survive had forged a fiery determination in these Ulster men and women. They now had to make a choice. What they had was good enough... much better than in the Old World. But something inside them said there was more. There just may be *real* freedom and bounty in that splendid, sprawling sod beyond the mountains. They needed to make the turn. Their point of pain pressed them to a decision to take that journey through The Gap and then make another turn southward into the long, lush valley below.

And when they did, oh what they saw. Hillsides that billowed like waves on the sea. Bluffs that braced up to heights and bent down to tree lines. Acres of fertile soil from which their sons would pull their potatoes. Fields to be creased by cornrows or left for livestock. It must have seemed a milk-and-honey land to them. Their hard work here could build a good life for generations.

If you've been to Ireland or Scotland, you can understand why they wanted to settle in Appalachia. They must have thought someone plucked the Scottish Highlands up and plopped them down right here in the New World. The turn they made changed everything for these pioneers and their sons and daughters after them.

The Valley of Decision

My personal journey of grief brings me often to a valley of decision. Each time I come to the Y in the road, I face a choice. Will I allow my anger and confusion to push me away from God, or will I answer, like the disciples, "To whom else shall we go? You have the words of life" (John 6:68)? The lament Psalms are a maze of guttural emotions, dead ends and decisions to turn. There is a turn toward God in every one of them.

The Turn starts with the decision to look square in the face of your pain, call it what it is, and not run from it. There is no "right way" to grieve, for we all respond and learn to cope differently. But there is a wrong way to grieve. If we don't face and embrace our emotions, we're more likely to get depressed, struggle with destructive anger, develop eating disorders... all kinds of maladies. If we stuff it down, it will come out another way, always a negative result.

I can slink back into my shell, lash out at the world, or look to the only real source of life. I have learned I can't run from the pain because the pain is inside me. I take it wherever I go, so I will encounter it all again elsewhere. If I harden myself against the trial, nothing positive can come from it. Turning toward God is the only way to health, and the laments show us the way.

But how do I know I will turn to God when a hard time comes? How can I be so sure I won't do like I've seen others do and run away from God to destructive habits and poor life choices? Hole up like a badger and sulk? Turn inward to the slow suicide of bitterness?

I've come to believe much of the decision happens before your time of testing. Wise decisions don't just appear from nowhere. They are worked into life over a history of walking daily with our Father. What we do in our day-to-day life with God will make the difference in our times of grief.

Coming to know Him in degrees, however small and insignificant those degrees seem, and choosing to seek to know God daily is where the decisions are actually made. When your life is severely shaken and every expectation is crushed, one of two things will slosh out: an orphan heart or the heart of a beloved child.

Sons, Daughters, and Orphans

In Psalm 142, David's lament flows from the fact that he is hiding in a cave, running for his life because King Saul is hunting him down like an animal to kill him. Saul is a classic example of an orphan-hearted man. Self-centered and independent, his identity is tied up in what people think of him. His self-worth is based on his performance. His orphan heart was driven by jealousy of David and fear that he would lose his kingdom to him. When his world was falling apart, he made a series of bad decisions that hurt him and those around him.

David, though, had a heart that delighted in his Heavenly Father. It was easier for him to trust and rest because he knew the character of his God. He was found worshiping in his highest moments and his lowest moments. He worshiped when facing fear and danger. He worshiped in the way he sought God's will and direction for his life. He worshiped even when repenting for his sin. And all of this is recorded in the lamenting Psalms.

Reactions like this don't just happen. They are forged in the furnace of a secret life with God. David's relationship with God wasn't only public; actually, it was mostly private. Saul's men discovered him, not because he was touring Palestine with his worship band, but because he was singing his songs to his sheep (see 1 Sam. 16:18–20). Looking up to the stars, marveling, wondering why the Maker of the heavens would think of him. Looking down at his flock and realizing that just as he cared for them, Yahweh cared for him.

No one is suddenly different from his or her established habits. David didn't randomly become the kind of man who would respond correctly in his valley of weeping. His life and habits were formed from his personal walk with God. He knew God to be a refuge and a provider, so in his despair, running for his life, he could turn to Him:

I cry to you, O Lord;
I say, "You are my refuge,
my portion in the land of the living.
—Psalm 142:5

My Turn

The morning I stood on my back deck under the weight of months of accumulated pain and burden—having watched the one person who mattered most to me on earth suffer and wane and grimace in pain, having borne the burden of a caretaker and in the end suffered a radical amputation of part of my soul—that morning, solely by God's grace, I made the Turn.

I lifted my eyes to my Father, bathed in the morning sunlight, picked up my guitar, and sang the song Melissa and I had sung together over and over those last months. I remembered.

We had first met in a context of worship, and music was a constant in our marriage. We led worship together for thirty-five years in many contexts and countries. It was one of the ways we connected most deeply. Now we were sitting together in those oversized chairs in the house we'd built together all those years ago. My favorite voice, her voice, had grown weaker—sometimes she could only mouth the words, but still she sang. Holding her once strong but now feeble hand—the hand that bore my ring, caressed the faces of our children, and performed one hundred thousand labors of love for her family—I remembered.

I remembered. We sang together as we had for decades; this time a song about the goodness of God, His faithfulness, His presence. It was the anthem of our life together. Our harmonies swelled, bouncing off the cathedral ceiling and the hardwood floors, amplifying our voices above the noises of cancer and care—a declaration that even now, He is good.

Now I stand alone...singing solo, but the truth of the song still stands. It is my personal psalm of lament. I could lean into my Father because I know *who* He is, despite my circumstances. I know He is kind, even when I don't see His kindness. It is natural to want to understand why things happen because we feel like that gives us some control. But peace that goes beyond understanding can come when I am willing to give up my right to understand and trust anyway.

The Turn is like the instinct of a newborn. Our first sound is a cry for help, a plea for what is beyond us that we somehow know we need but cannot give ourselves. We are pushed from the womb lamenting from mothers who are also lamenting the pain and distress that is bringing new life.

Every time we lean toward God, we respond to a love that is unconditional and never-ending. I found that in my grief experience, it was not so much about my will or ability to turn to God, but His heart of love that first turned to me and drew me to himself. It takes courage to shift ourselves Godward, but the fount of that courage is not us, it is Him. So turning, in the end, is all of the courage with none of the pride.

I don't know why Melissa died. We had enough prayer going up for her from faith-filled, miracle-believing Christians that half the earth should have been healed. But she wasn't… at least not on earth, and we were praying for an earthly healing. When you are in the middle of that loss, or when something triggers your feeling of loss, there is a temptation to run to false comforts that are only temporary and don't really help us. We look to food or substances or entertainment or gratifying our sinful desires to help ease our pain. But that is for orphans. Sons and daughters turn to their Father.

When I was on my sabbatical, trying to find my bearings in the whirlwind of emotions, it occurred to me that there are only two options. I could get stuck in my grief or not get stuck in my grief. I understand why people feel paralyzed. The pain of emotional trauma can be crippling. I will never again judge someone who can't see a way forward, for I have been there. But I began to see that getting stuck doesn't help anyone. It doesn't honor Melissa. It doesn't honor God. It doesn't help my children or me or the people around me. So there's really only one option: go forward. The problem is I don't know how to do that. So I turn to God. And still, I return to Him every day through this gift of lament.

Blessed

Jesus, in the sermon that introduced the culture of heaven to earth, stood before poor and desperate people living under the oppression of a foreign government and declared that they are blessed if they are poor in Spirit (see Matt. 5:3). When we are at the end of our own resources, we are blessed because there is a spring of supply that is available to us. Even in this wanting world, the resources of heaven are ours.

And then He said—think of it—we are blessed when we mourn (see Matt. 5:4). Though it sounds crazy, mourning is the only way to know the treasure of His comfort. In our darkest time, He faces us, opens His arms to us, He welcomes us, and He fights for us when we are unable to fight.

When the early settlers were learning to navigate the rolling rivers of East Tennessee, they found out quickly that the current can be unpredictable and that flow can change rapidly. They learned that regardless of the changing direction of the water's flow, they could turn their oars to an angle that would work with the contrary currents and steer the boats in the desired direction. And so it is with grief—we can't control the events of our life, but we can control the turn of our oar.

So we turn to God; but what next? Like the newborn, pushed from the pelvis of our grief into a new and uncharted world, bloody and cold and dependent...we cry out.

Wisdom from the School of Sorrow

Giving yourself permission to grieve

Grief is the natural result of the love that you had—sort of a price tag that shows value and cost. Your person is worth the pain and worth celebrating. It is important to give yourself and others around you permission to grieve…as long as and in whatever way they need.

There may be expectations that after a period of time has passed, you should be beyond a certain point in your grief. But that isn't necessarily true. If you feel that pressure, you can begin to start hiding your grief and not sharing it as much with others. In some cultures, it is easier and more acceptable to grieve openly or for longer periods of time.

There's often a stigma among our family or close friends that we should "be strong" and always be on top of it all. That can be very hard when we find ourselves in a place of feeling undone or lost. Sometimes we are preoccupied with care or funeral issues or just everyday life. This may cause us to delay or alter our grieving.

Allowing ourselves to feel the real, painful, and shameful parts and bring them to God can help keep us sane.

Quote:

I had a miscarriage and instead of grieving I just went numb. I ended up going to a talk by a woman who spoke on grieving. I went up to talk to her afterwards about my inability to grieve. She prayed for me. I went home, climbed into bed in the middle of the day and basically slept for twenty-four hours. And it broke the dam and brought me to a better place. I know that grieving is necessary but due to my particular life story, I find it very difficult and I wish I had more encouragement from others in this area. (E. H.)

CHAPTER FOUR

The Cry

Incline your ear,
O Lord, and answer me,
for I am poor and needy.
—Psalm 86:1

On the trail, pumping pedals jumpstart a melody in my mind and, I can't help it, a song rises up in me. Music has always been deep in my bones. I can't walk down a hall or pedal on a path without a song springing up. Today it's the hymn "Great Is Thy Faithfulness." Yeah, the one she walked down the aisle to on our wedding day.

The steady pulse strengthens my climb up the wood-lined ridge and I realize again there is a rhythm in the forest here too. It is constant but not consistent. It's more constant than any of us, for generations have come and gone with its cadence. But it changes minute by minute:

the wobble of the warbler's song, the percussion of the woodpecker, the harmony of the waters, singing as they fall over the rocks that slow the stream. In the forest, I am serenaded by a symphony of wind-blown leaves and crescendoing cicadas. You can even hear the sound of the heat on a steamy summer day.

There is rhythm down in the very sod of this valley. In fact, I'd say music may be the strongest contribution of our area to the girth of humanity. The real, raw, marrow-deep issues of our lives have always been brought out in our music: birth, death, love, longing, loss, redemption—all the *brutifulness* of life laid on a plate before you—served with a haunting melody and heavenly harmonies. This is why country music and its cousin, bluegrass, are so popular throughout the world. They offer real emotions about real issues from real lives played on real instruments.

Melissa's grandparents lived a ridge apart from each other here in what is now Cherokee National Forest. The valley that separated them was filled with corn and beans and sweat and blisters. On Saturday nights, their families would gather to make music, sing, and dance. This was their Netflix, their Spotify. It was the artistic release of the week's hard work, and hardened hands would clap and chord and join together in squares on the floor. On one such occasion a young couple's eyes caught and lingered, and that glance sparked a sixty-year marriage. Two generations later my treasure was born.

The music they played was rooted in Ulster and the Scottish Highlands. Jigs and reels and, oh those ballads, those haunting, heartbreaking ballads. This music is not about tone trends, or hype, or a three-minute radio hook that sells millions. It's about the mad, sad, glad, and bad of life; the whole *brutiful* breadth of human experience.

Most of them learned to sing in church. Just like David of old, the songs and hymns they wrote and sang communicated their struggle and their hope for a better day ahead. The same can be said about the influence of the music of our African brothers and sisters. Particularly in the western part of our state, their cries were the roots of blues, jazz, and rock and roll. Songs of lament are as old and varied as humanity.

It is from the ground of these common human experiences, across time and ocean alike, that the cry of these mountain songs was mined. In them, we find a connection to our own grief. We can hear in the cry of the Psalmist an echo of our own personal pain.

East Tennessee is known as the birthplace and cradle of country music, which was born and nurtured here before moving on to Nashville, a city with a more powerful radio station. Artists like The Carter Family,

Roy Acuff, Chet Atkins, Dolly Parton, and the Everly Brothers were the faces of the soul of these parts.

If there is one theme that is constant in these songs—whether from Ireland or Appalachia—it is longing. They are the artistic expression of the cry of the human heart, a recognition of our needs and our limitations. They are an admission of things we cannot control. Many of them are modern-day psalms of lament. In their essence, they are prayers.

In some ways prayer is natural to us. Through prayer we reach out beyond ourselves for what we need: love, well-being, wholeness, hope, and salvation.

Being poor in spirit involves a recognition of our smallness, that we are made from dust, and we hold this treasure of the image of God in jars of clay. Clay jars are just dirt mixed with water, molded by pressure, and passed through fire. In the cry of lament, we admit that life is fragile, and we are needy.

The people of East Tennessee are no strangers to poverty. My own mother was the youngest of twelve children growing up on a farm on the rolling hills of Jefferson County. They lived in a small and simple house, clearing the land in order to grow their crops. They raised their own chickens, hogs, and cattle; they cured their own meat and stored it for hard times. Canned fruits and vegetables filled the cellar under the house. Milk and butter, honey and molasses, lye soap, furniture, and clothing: they grew or made or traded for everything they needed to survive. Though there was no doctor nearby, they knew the herbs and plants that could cure illnesses. Their toilet and water source were outside.

If my mother grew up country poor, my dad grew up city poor. It was not the fault of his father, for my grandpa was a carpenter, fireman, and custodian; he was anything he could be in order to make it through the Great Depression. My dad told me of the time his father was paid for a carpentering job with two bushel baskets of turnips. The family ate turnips for two weeks; it was all they had. Till his dying day, my dad never ate another turnip. Melissa's family had a similar history. But despite their humble beginnings, both our families worked hard, took advantage of their opportunities, and made a good life for us.

I've been to enough desolate places on this earth to know that poverty is not a blessing. It is a curse. But there is a blessing held out for those who are poor in spirit: a strength in weakness, a kind provision, eyes to see what is most important. There is a cry in the soul of this East Tennessee valley. There is a cry in the valley of weeping too.

Being Real with God

If the first step on the lamenting journey is turning to God, the second step is crying out. It is having the boldness to be blatantly honest and say exactly what you are feeling before the God of the universe. Hebrew Scholar Chad Bird, in his wonderful devotional *Unveiling Mercy,* gives us a hint of the deep cry that emerges from the very first word of the book of Lamentations:

> *How lonely sits the city*
> *that was full of people!*
> *How like a widow has she become,*
> *she who was great among the nations!*
> *She who was a princess among the provinces*
> *has become a slave.*
> —Lamentations 1:1

Chad Bird explains:

> *The Hebrew name for Lamentations is Eykah, its opening word [How]. It's a gut-wrenching wail stretched in the rack of ruin. Tears become ink in this book, penned with cruciform calligraphy. Translating Eykah as "how" just seems too bland. The word needs to burn the mouth as it is spoken, baptizing the tongue with ashes, for it erupts from a heart torched by grief. Alas, Jerusalem, Jerusalem, the princess now*

a slave, the wife now widow, the living now coffined city of God.

This book is just as important for what it says as for what its very existence shows: that God's ears and heart are open to lament. We are given permission—indeed, blessing—to weep, wail, and moan our way toward healing. Faith necessitates no stiff upper lip. Jesus wept. So do we. While we grieve, our Lord of love will never walk away.[3]

He's right. "How could this happen?" is the cry of many in the Bible. The weeping prophets and the psalmists say things to God many of us would be afraid to say:

I thought you were faithful, but
you're not. Look at my life…
obviously you've abandoned me.
How long, O Lord? Will you forget
me forever? Others are thriving
while we, your people, are dying by bits.
All my life I have served you…
it has all been for nothing.

---

3 Chad Bird, *Unveiling Mercy: 365 Daily Devotions Based on Insights from Old Testament Hebrew.* (Irvine: 1517 Publishing, 2020), 324.

My enemies surround me and drain my hope from me.

In his distress, David cries out to God over a dozen times in Psalm 86. In his cries, he calls God by all three of his Hebrew names:

"O Jehovah...hear me"
"O Elohim...save me"
"O Adonai...be merciful to me"
—Psalms 86:1–17

David understands his situation as in effect he calls out:

Almighty God, if you don't see me,
hear me, rescue me...I have no hope.

This is what happens when we make The Turn. We see, we understand our own poverty, and we cry out. In another song of lament, David pours out his guilty soul after his adultery with Bathsheba and the murder of her husband, Uriah. With the great insight that comes to a broken man in the School of Sorrow, he teaches us a truth about God:

Behold, you delight in truth in the inner being,
and you teach me wisdom in the secret heart.
—Psalm 51:6

Later in the song, David in effect says to God, if you wanted a bull or a lamb, I would cut it open right here. But you want my heart (see Ps. 51). It's much easier to cut open a bull than to cut open our wounded hearts and bare them all before the Lord. But our honesty is beautiful to God.

The Real Sacrifice

God wants us to be real because he wants us to heal. He is not upset by our emotions nor intimidated by our accusations. It is easy for us to believe that our cries to God demonstrate unbelief. If we are not happy, there must be something wrong with our faith. In reality, our prayers of complaint are true prayers of faith. Maybe they are the highest form of faith because we are feeling the weight of the brokenness of this world, and yet we turn to God and cry to Him.

I've had my own questions:

What do I do with these
recurring waves of sorrow?
Who am I now in light of this great loss?
How long will my life be defined
by what I have lost?

Prayers are not always polite. In our worst times, the Psalms give us the freedom to go ahead and say what we are feeling. They even give us the words to pray when we can't find our own. Of course, an all-knowing God already knows what we are feeling and thinking. So why is it important to be honest and say it? Because when we name what we feel—when we come clean before God—He can begin to give us his perspective.

My Hinge

On my grief journey, an unexpected and powerful lesson of lament happened to me on a long walk around a lake in Georgia. Brisk morning air gripped my skin as I walked the trail that outlined the lake. Light shimmered off the water and patchy reds and yellows of autumn were waving with the wind—a sense of expectancy, of something inside wanting to surface. I had come to understand that moving my body and drinking in nature were part of my healing journey. But I also knew I needed to speak honestly with God, so I decided the best way to start was to make a list of the things I had lost when I lost Melissa.

It was a very long list.

I lost my best friend.
My lover.
My confidant.

I lost the beauty of her face.
The sound of her voice.

Her encouraging words.

Her wisdom.

Her rebukes.

Her balance to me.

I lost her charm without deceit,

her beauty without vanity.

I lost the main source of joy I have on this earth.

I lost the one who knew me best and still loved me.

The one God gave me to complete me.

The best mother my children could have known.

I lost the hand I used to hold in worship.

Her meals.

Her care.

Her kiss.

All the dreams we dreamt together that died with her.

And infinitely more.

The model of lament in the Psalms gave me the courage to turn to God and lay it all on the line; it gave me the courage to pour out my pain and loss. I walked for hours down rocky paths and backroads. I lifted my complaint from a throat made hoarse by ragweed and raging. From lonely docks, my groans of pain echoed off the waters to heaven. I shook my list of losses in the face of God and asked Him to show me the justice in my wife's death.

It was raw and real and emotionally exhausting, and in the end, I felt a measure of relief just getting it out. Then something very significant happened. I sensed the inner voice of the Holy Spirit speaking, "Go back down the same list, line for line, and thank me for giving these things to you."

His voice took my breath. I stopped, stunned in my tracks. It felt as though the world around me stopped too. This was such a change in perspective it felt like emotional whiplash. Thank Him? I never would have thought of it on my own, at least not at that time. But this wasn't a harsh voice; it wasn't a rebuke. It was a gentle shepherding of my wounded soul, a tender "this is the way...walk in it."

Is this even possible? My mind had been so consumed by what I had lost. Of course it had. That is normal; that is what grief does to you. But my mind went to the words of a book I had just read, written by another man who had lost his wife to cancer. In his grief journal, penned after his wife Joy died, C. S. Lewis had written, "The pain I feel now is the happiness I had before. That's the deal."[4]

Job said it even straighter:

---

4 C.S. Lewis, *A Grief Observed* (HarperOne, 2015).

"The Lord gave,
and the Lord has taken away;
blessed be the name of the Lord."
—Job 1:21

I winced and caught my breath again. But I know the voice of my Father. Though this doesn't make sense, He wouldn't steer me wrong. So I started.

God, I *thank you* for giving me a best friend as my wife.
God, I *thank you* for giving me one who knew me best and loved me most.
God, I *thank you* for the hand I held as we worshiped.
God, I *thank you* for such a wonderful wife for my children…

As I went down the list—all the way down it—a wave of brokenness washed over me and then a wave of healing. But the healing didn't replace the brokenness. It covered it and mingled with it. The pain didn't disappear, but a new way of seeing came to me. As I let the pain of my loss push me into thankfulness for what I had been given, I was able to make my way, like Job, to *blessed be the Name of the Lord.*

Why would my tender Shepherd guide me out of my pit of loss by telling me to be grateful? Because grief is a thief. It tries to steal the joy of the beautiful life Melissa and I had together. It numbs my heart so I don't fully experience the grace of God today. It wants to get its thieving hands on any hope for my future. The only cure I have found for moments of grief is gratitude. And I repeat this lesson, learned in the School of Sorrow, every day. Feel what you feel, celebrate what you had, and praise the Lord: *"Oh God, what I've lost... but oh God, what you gave me...Blessed be your Name."*

There are waves of desperate sadness. Oftentimes I feel like I'm tumbling in the waves of grief, but I am tethered. I am held fast by my Man of Sorrows. The tears are always in the reservoir, waiting for a trigger, a thought, a memory to brim them over:

- Waking up every day in the house Melissa and I built together.
- Walking into the coffee shop where we sat for hours planning that anniversary trip—the one she dreamt of for years, the one we were just weeks away from when the diagnosis came.
- My grandson looking up from the truck he is playing with weeks after her death with the question, "Where's Mimi?"

There is nowhere I can go where there is no trigger. But the pain of loss can press me into joy for all we had. Walking through this step of lament has released me to celebrate what Melissa and I had together, not merely mourn her loss. She is worth celebrating, so I have learned to fully go there. I have to cry out. I have to allow the Holy Spirit to guide me *into* these emotions so He can guide me *through* them in a healthy way.

Sitting with our Grief

In Appalachia, when family or close friends died, the custom was to sit up with the dead. Just as the Jews "sit shiva," my ancestors had a mourning period for the immediate family of the deceased that created a space of comfort and community for mourners. With no funeral homes, the deceased were kept at home until burial. In those days, the women prepared the body by stretching it out on a "laying out" board made from slabs of wood or a door laid on top of two sawhorses. While women washed and dressed the body, men hand-dug the grave. This very personal, hands-on care was a final expression of love for the departed.

Each death was an intimate community event—a church bell would toll announcing the death, ringing once for every year of the person's life. Everyone within hearing distance could count the tolls and guess who might have died. Neighbors, friends, and family, with food in hand, would gather at the home to comfort the grieving family. Close friends and family would stay all night—sitting up with the dead.

I write this because there is a lesson for us here. If grief is a revealer and a source of wisdom, we don't need to turn away from it but rather pay attention to it. We need to sit with our grief. Our pain can lead us along the pathway of lament where we will find healing and hope. Dealing honestly with our emotions is a crucial part of our healing. We may never fully realize our potential as persons and followers of Jesus if we don't sit with our grief and allow God to guide us through the valley of weeping.

A Mantle of Kindness

One of my prayers since Melissa's death has been that I might have a small bit of her kindness. Everyone who knew her would describe her as a kind friend who always saw you and cared about what was going on in your life. It was the beautiful fruit of Jesus that poured through her. I would love to have more of that in my life.

In the crucible of chronic illness, or an untimely death, or a broken marriage, or the fog of unrealized expectations—what is truly on the inside of a person makes its way to the surface. In the throes of the final stages of pancreatic cancer, what came out of Melissa was the most beautiful thing I've seen on this earth. Even in her weakness, hers was the bravest, purest, most selfless display of the kindness of Jesus I have ever seen, shown in many deeds to many people. Let me tell you about one of them.

Two weeks before Melissa died, she finished her seventh chemotherapy regimen. Each regimen consisted of three days of chemo treatments per week for three consecutive weeks. When undergoing chemotherapy, a drug or a blend of drugs is introduced into your body in an effort to kill cancer cells. The treatment is systemic, so the effects occur throughout the entire body. The cure becomes the curse as horrible side effects begin to manifest.

Melissa had experienced the loss of her hair, nausea, anemia, extreme fatigue, neuropathy, mouth sores, digestion problems, pain, and many other effects from the chemicals. It is difficult to explain the process of receiving treatment. The infusion room is very cold. The natural anxiety over injecting poisons into your body grates on you. You are not feeling well, and you know this is going to make you feel worse. It is important to remember that many are helped by these treatments, but still, they are in no way easy. And although the medical staff was sympathetic and very professional, the entire experience is very unnerving.

On the final day of her three-day treatment, we met a couple, maybe in their seventies, who were checking into the cancer center for the first time. The husband was undergoing his first treatment, perhaps the most unsettling and fearful thing he had ever experienced. Melissa spoke her kind words and helped him understand what he was about to face.

When Melissa finished her treatment, I went outside to pull the car around to pick her up. She walked from the cold, sterile treatment facility into the bright autumn sunshine. The man's wife was sitting in the warmth of the sun on a bench, and I saw my beautiful bride—two weeks from her death, suffering from stage four, metastatic pancreatic cancer, having just been pumped full of poison on the off chance that it would cure her—open the door, notice the lady there on the bench, stop, turn, and walk over to her. She introduced herself, explained some things that could help with practical issues, and gave some tips to best navigate their journey of treatment. Her considerate words brought comfort and peace to the elderly woman. This was my Melissa.

Her bucket was kicked and out came Jesus. I could tell many such stories of Melissa's last days... always thinking of others, always concerned with what concerned them, always ready with a kind word. I have made it my prayer since her death that I might walk in a small degree of her kindness. Of course, I know I am really asking for the fruit of the Spirit. I am really asking for the heart of Jesus. That is what she carried within her to the end.

But I will never be able to have her kindness without facing my brokenness and allowing God to mend it. Only by turning to the source of healing and receiving love from God will I ever be able to see that prayer answered.

Bring Your Wounds

Oftentimes when we come to worship, our minds say we should leave the cares outside the door. But the Psalms teach us to bring our burdens in and let them *become* our worship. Bringing brokenness to God is beautiful and costly worship. It is strong faith.

When we are grieving loss of any kind, the One who has lost more than any of us will faithfully guide us. No one out-suffers Christ. The Man of Sorrows welcomes us into his heart and into fellowship with his sufferings in the midst of our pain. He knows exactly how to comfort us.

Three times David calls out to God using three different names in Psalm 86. And three times the key attribute of God's character is revealed to him through an untranslatable word and unfathomable love. This revelation is the third step in biblical lament. And what we see when we turn, cry, and draw near to him will take our breath away.

Wisdom from the School of Sorrow

Men and Grieving

Grief can be tough for men for several reasons. Our culture (and perhaps our families of origin) may have taught us that crying is a form of weakness. This creates a habit of pushing difficult feelings down instead of facing and feeling them. Men may attempt to be rational or to try to be in control and courageous. This may ironically lead to irrational thinking, irritability/anger issues, and depression. Of course, silence and withdrawal can also be valid expressions of grief, but isolation can be dangerous.

Men may desire to protect their family, so they do not allow themselves (or others) to feel the natural pain of loss. They may make attempts to remove grief or move on from their pain quickly, throwing themselves into projects to avoid dealing with what they feel.

Men and women seem to deal with grief differently, partially because of biological differences in brain structure. While women tend to process their grief emotionally and verbally, men will usually be more logical than emotional. But the absence of tears doesn't equal the absence of pain.

These are generalizations and depend on many variables, such as the level of self-awareness and the level of support from family and friends. But these pressures, when combined with the grief we feel, can be confusing and seem overwhelming. Overall, the pathway through lament that we see in the Psalms is a powerful way for men to find hope in their grief.

Quote:

I think men may grieve just as deeply but choose to do so privately. I don't know if that is necessarily a bad thing because if you look at how Jesus dealt with grief, he did both. My default has been to grieve privately. The one exception came during the unexpected death of my father. My in-laws, who were out of town at the time, were not able to get with us until the next day. Upon their arrival, my father-in-law came straight to me, embraced me, and began weeping as if he had just lost his dad. His genuine expression of sorrow enabled me to feel safe enough to grieve publicly during that moment. But once it was over, I went back to privately working through it. (Scott B.)

CHAPTER FIVE

The Reveal

Deep calls to deep at the roar of your
waterfalls: all your breakers and your
waves have gone over me.
By day the Lord commands his steadfast love,
and at night his song is with me,
a prayer to the God of my life.
—Psalms 42:7–8

Riding the winding, wooded path, the fall colors are beginning to seep through the greenery, and I'm reminded why I love this part of the world. In East Tennessee, we are blessed with four distinct seasons each year. It's magical and magnificent.

In winter the sun hangs low, glinting orange over frost-bitten mountains. Snow, when it comes, covers and cleans, insulates and imposes a silence on the woodlands, its beauty luring you in to explore, if you dare. The dormant, leafless trees sharpen the outline of the ridges and valleys with greater clarity. Everything waits, latent with possibility.

Spring bursts forth in blooms—1,500 types of flowering plants here—delicate star chickweed, yellow trillium, bloodroot, stonecrop, and violets of purple and yellow. Farmland shifts from a pale to a brighter shade of green or to gold, waving field grass beneath clouds of dogwood blooms nestled against a sea of evergreen. Swelling streams, the spillover of snow-capped mountains ramble over rocks and sing an endless song.

In summer, the morning fog lifts off the one thousand square miles of water surface in the Tennessee Valley—a mecca for those who kayak, fish, swim, and ski. Verdant green hillsides soak in the sun while in the highlands a sea of smoky blue mist rises, creating the appearance of fire on the mountains. A birder's paradise, a hiker's dream, fungi and ferns, salamanders and snakes, birds, bats, and bears. Life everywhere.

Ah, but fall tops it all. Summer haze begins to clear as the valley cools under flocks of migrating birds. Squirrels scurry and turkeys toddle, gorging, gathering, and getting ready for the greying days that lie ahead. Fall splashes color on the creases of our ridges and dapples the hilled farmland with hues like an impressionist's painting, floating clouds filtering the tint and tone of the canvas minute by minute.

I dare you not to awe.

Above all, it is the trees that hold for us revelation. Myriad deciduous trees mark the turning of the seasons with barren branches, then pale buds, then densely packed green leaves, and at last vibrant red, orange, and yellow fire in fall. Each season foretelling, then unveiling another layer of the life and creativity of the Maker.

Unveiling

In the School of Sorrow, there is also an unveiling. Nothing reveals the heart of the student or the Teacher more than lament. Psalm 42 is life and lament at its highest and lowest, all in one twisting, trailing song. This psalm has some of our most beloved quotes—the ones we see on pretty plaques and memes. But it also has verses we will never see on a plaque or meme. The clash of worlds, internal and external, is so evident here it leaves us wondering. In grief, there is something you need to know that no mortal's book can tell you. The Father must reveal it.

In the superscription of Psalm 42, we see it is a *maskil of the Sons of Korah*. Maskil is a musical term of uncertain meaning, but many scholars suggest that it carries a connotation of teaching—a song that holds instruction for life. If so, what can we learn from this brave, baffling ballad?

Music is all about tension and release. A good piece of music swells and sinks with changing dynamics that provide its sway over our emotions. If that is what makes a good song, we could call this one a great song. We don't know what the music sounded like, but the lyrics alone are a perfect symphony of emotions.

In the lyrics of this ancient hymn I see, in this order and in rapid succession, these emotions:

deep longing
expectation
tears
fear of abandonment
a poured-out soul
fond remembering
glad shouts
praise songs
self-encouragement
hope
hopelessness
conversation with the deep of God
waves that overtake me
the steadfast love of God
prayer to the God of my life
abandonment

mourning
oppression of the enemy
wounds to my bones
shouts of my enemies
remembering hope
fresh revelation of God, my salvation.
Welcome to the world of lament.

It begs the question, were the Sons of Korah bipolar? Unstable? Or maybe they were just realistic. These are the familiar waves of grief, and over and over in the Psalms of Lament we see a recurring miracle. When the darkness is blackest, the God of Glory stoops and stills and reveals himself. Powerful, loving, faithful, Creator, strong, wise, long-suffering, truthful, unchanging, Sovereign Lord, shepherd...in nearly every sad song there is a fresh revelation of who He is:

But you, O Lord, are a shield about me (Ps. 3:3).
But you are my strong refuge (Ps. 71:7).
Yet you are holy (Ps. 22:3).

And there are also fresh reminders of what he has done.

But you have saved us from our foes (Ps. 44:7).

Yet God my King is from old, working salvation in the midst of the earth (Ps. 74:12).

Yet you have brought us out to a place of abundance (Ps. 66:12).

Remember who He is. Remember what He has done. And in this way, we begin to know Him deeper than ever before. In our deepest pain, there are *buts* and *yets*. Still, the key revelation in this psalm, and the key to all laments, is found right in the middle.

By day the Lord commands his steadfast love,
and at night his song is with me,
A prayer to the God of my life.
—Psalm 42:8

Carried by Kindness

Steadfast love. The key word is *hesed*—the undefinable Hebrew word that tries to describe the indescribable loving heart of God. *Hesed* is eternal and limitless love, kindness, compassion, grace, mercy, faithfulness, and here, steadfast love. But it goes beyond being a characterization of the nature of God. *Hesed* love is a loyalty that moves God to action on our behalf. It is both his heart for us and his hand toward us. And it is Love's call that initiates a response from us.

Michael Card, in his groundbreaking book *Inexpressible*, points out that linguists have found no cognate in any other language that can directly translate *hesed.* [5] The King James Version uses fourteen different words or word combinations to try to convey its meaning. It is uniquely Hebrew because it is unique to the Hebrew God, and no one is like him. In all surrounding cultures, as far as we know, the concept of a God like this never existed.

Card offers his own definition of this ultimately undefinable word: Hesed is *when the one from whom I have the right to expect nothing gives me everything.*[6]

This is our God…unfathomably beautiful. *Hesed* appears 250 times in the Old Testament, 127 of those are in the Psalms. We see it constantly in the lamenting Psalms, especially those written by David. In fact, it is the perceived absence of *hesed* that is being lamented in these Psalms—the sense that God is *not* compassionate, *not* faithful in his covenant, *not* present with us. That is the tension we feel in the Bible's laments. That is also the tension we feel in our own grief and loss.

In the midst of his own wilderness, Moses asked God to reveal his glory to him. God hid Moses, covered

5 Michael Card, *Inexpressible: Hesed and the Mystery of God's Lovingness*. (IVP. 2018), 5.
6 Michael Card, *Inexpressible: Hesed and the Mystery of God's Lovingness*. (IVP. 2018), 324.

him with His hand and showed him his goodness, his kindness, his *hesed*. Here is God's revelation of his own heart and nature to Moses and to us:

> *The Lord passed before him and proclaimed, "The Lord, the Lord, a God merciful and gracious, slow to anger, and abounding in steadfast love [hesed] and faithfulness, keeping steadfast love [hesed] for thousands, forgiving iniquity and transgression and sin, but who will by no means clear the guilty, visiting the iniquity of the fathers on the children and the children's children, to the third and the fourth generation."*
> *—Exodus 34:6–7*

This exact description is repeated three times in Psalms 86:15, 103:7–10, and 145:8–9. It is closely related to God's covenant with his chosen people, Israel, but it is expressed in human form in the New Testament in the person and ministry of Jesus Christ. This is what sets our God apart from all others. Not only that he is sovereign or all-powerful or perfectly holy, but that he is kind.

He is kind.

In the vortex of emotions mourned out in this psalm, the revelation of the kindness of God leads to the question,

Why are you cast down, O my soul,
and why are you in turmoil within me?
Hope in God; for I shall again praise him,
my salvation
—Psalms 42:5,11

Kindness and hope. These are the revelations and the results of walking the journey of lament. This is what we learn in the School of Sorrow.

Kindness in chaos

Finding the *hesed* of God in my pit of grief saved me. I didn't realize the pit is the very best place to find his kindness. In Psalm 32, we see David in deep despair, his enemies taking counsel together, scheming to find the best way to end his life. Then we read these words:

Blessed be the Lord,
for he has wondrously shown
his steadfast love to me
when I was in a besieged city.
—Psalm 31:21

This makes no sense at all. A besieged city is surrounded by the enemy, cut off from the rest of the world, a city with a past but no future. No food, no water, no hope... just waiting to die. But that is precisely where David said God's *hesed* became a wonder to him. God shone a light on His love, mercy, and faithfulness so that David experienced the revelation that changed everything for him.

Here is what I have learned and what I want you to hear: we don't have to fear our darkest times. God our Father is there with his *hesed* love. In our deep grief, presence is our greatest need—to know God is near. The place we find the assurance of His nearness is lament.

I have a spiritual discipline of journaling each year. I don't journal every experience of every day, but I usually fill a writing journal during the course of the year with what I feel God may be speaking, teaching, or correcting in my life. One of my favorite times of the year is the last week of December when I look over the previous year and choose the top five things I believe God has taught me. I do this because I don't want to forget what he has spoken.

The only problem is the year Melissa was diagnosed, suffered, and died was the worst year of my life. The last thing I wanted to do was look back over that year. I was beginning to learn the groove of presenting my pain to God and learning how to manage my triggers. But still, at times, the deep and unexpected pains of loss would double me over. Although these brushes with grief-pain seemed to be growing shorter in duration and less frequent, when you are beginning to stabilize, you really don't want to rock the boat with fresh memories.

But a spiritual discipline is something you do whether or not you feel like it, and I somehow felt it would be important for my journey. So bracing myself and embracing the grace of my Father, I poured through the pages and relived my year, which included an extra journal I wrote on my sabbatical, taken the month after Melissa died. As I stepped into this fearful place, I had no idea of the beauty and kindness I would discover.

Reading those journals—reliving those moments—I remembered the vision I had while praying with some friends before my sabbatical after Melissa's death. In my mind, I saw a picture of my Heavenly Father with a calm, assured, and confident face—as if He had a specific plan for this sabbatical. Then, I saw what I understood to be the Holy Spirit dressed in the outfit of a guide on safari or expedition: khaki shirt, safari pants, and hat; binoculars, knife, and coiled rope... as if He was equipped with everything needed to guide me on this journey. And I had a sense that Jesus, the Man of Sorrows, stood with gentle eyes and extended arms, ready to trade my burden for his. My God was everything I needed for my grieving journey. But He had also been everything we had needed the previous six months.

During those months before Melissa's homegoing, there were many trips to the ER and stays in the hospital. The emergency department was always full because of

COVID-19 restrictions at the time. Even though advanced cancer patients normally get some sort of priority in these situations, we often had to wait for hours in the hallway of the ER before we got a room where we could wait for a room in the hospital. I remember piling blankets on top of Melissa to try to keep her shivering body warm in the cold halls and rooms. The sound of monitors beeping, the rush of the doctors, and the communal suffering of all who were there. None of this was the fault of the hospital personnel. They were doing their best. But COVID-19 complicated and caused mayhem in many ways.

The twist in my soul and my stomach was caused by the difficulty in caring for and advocating for Melissa. We had no control over what was happening in her body or what was occurring because of the crisis in the hospital. Communication between medical professionals was muddied. Visits from family and friends were restricted, and we were very much alone during the weeks she spent in the hospital. It was a mental, emotional, and physical roller coaster.

When she was released, our days were punctuated with local trips to oncologists and trips to two national cancer centers. But most of our time during those months was spent at home, managing pain and the effects of the treatments Melissa was receiving. We had phone calls with traditional and holistic professionals and we struggled with the balance of finding the right regimen of supplements and treatments.

Despite the uncertainty of facing a new struggle we knew little about and a huge learning curve with nutrition and meds, there was something unexpected and much more powerful that overshadowed our days. There was a sense of overwhelming peace—as if our simple home had become the very sanctuary of God. Some of this came in the sense of God's presence—His shalom, in the truest sense of the word—within us and around us. Surprisingly, we found it possible to melt into God's protective arms, to relax and lean back into the goodness and mercy that follow us all the days of our lives (see Psalm 23:6).

But this peace also came in the form of the people who surrounded us during that time. The enticing aromas and sweet tastes filled our kitchen as Melissa's cousin Shannon drove hours to our house, often multiple times a week, to cook the food that Melissa needed for her special diet. The quiet and peaceful times when old friends came over to sit around the table or in the sun on the back deck and talk over old times. The pastoral visits from our fellow elders in the church strengthened our spirits.

A thousand small acts of kindness from those who wished they could do more but couldn't conceive how big their "small" service was to us. The frequent visits from our children and the many ways they showed love to their mom and me; the sound of the grandkid's laughter; the friend that sent a handwritten card *every day* for months in the mail, stamped and addressed and bearing an encouraging word and scripture. The gifts of money given to offset the expenses of the nontraditional treatments that were not covered by insurance. The messages from around the world from friends who were adding their petitions to the prayer furnace that was burning for Melissa. The overwhelming cumulative love and covering from the body of Christ is humbling and empowering.

Looking back over that most difficult year, I was astonished. Through every diagnosis, treatment, scan, and crying session; with all the questions and uncertainty; in all the pain of loss, the one word emblazoned like a banner over that year was *kindness*.

In the worst year of my life, I came to know His *hesed*. He was kind in His presence that was always with us. He was kind in his provision of all that we needed. He was kind through the body of Christ that held us up and extended their hands to help. He gave me everything I needed. He gave Melissa everything she needed. Even through my grieving process, His kind and loving hand has been ever-present. "*Though I walk through the valley…you are with me…goodness and hesed follow me all the days of my life.*"

Revealing God

This great, kind heart is what we see when we turn to God and cry out honestly to Him. But in the Reveal there is another turn: God turns toward us and He turns our eyes to see Him in fresh ways. There is a special kind of grace God gives us in the School of Sorrow: washed eyes to see Him clearer, brighter, bigger, deeper, and more accurately, and softened hearts to receive his love.

Some months after Melissa's death, I attended an exhibition featuring a multimedia presentation of the life and works of the famous impressionist painter Vincent Van Gogh. He was a man who experienced his own deep periods of sorrow and depression—including self-mutilation and suicide. Yet he had the ability to see things others did not see and replicate them on a genius level, leaving an artistic legacy few, if any, can compare with.

His famous painting *Starry Night,*[7] painted from his room in a mental asylum in southern France, has been valued at one hundred million dollars. Though a tragically disturbed man, van Gogh had a keen insight. A

7 Vincent van Gogh, *The Starry Night*, 1889, oil on canvas, 29 x 36 ¼", Museum of Modern Art, New York.

quote of his struck me: *"It often seems to me that night is still more richly colored than the day."*[8]

Indeed, he painted the night sky in many paintings using no black at all, only the deepest, most intense violets, blues, and greens. He was a rare human who could see the color in the dark of night. On my journey of grief, discovering the *hesed* of God, this was significant. For there are *hesed* hues that can only be seen in the dark night of the soul. Our God gives our dark night its boundaries; He dictates the seasons of grief. He reveals colors in the darkness.

> *Even the darkness is not dark to you;*
> *the night is as bright as the day;*
> *for darkness is as light with you*
> —Psalms 139:12

The God who Sees

A beautiful example of The Reveal comes to us from one of the darkest stories in scripture. Because of a dysfunctional relationship in the marriage of Abram and Sarai, Hagar (Sarai's servant girl), found herself forced to become pregnant with Abram's child. Contention and jealousy caused Sarai to abuse Hagar, forcing her to run away into the wilderness. With no way of providing for herself and her child, she lifted her lament to the Lord.

8 Vincent van Gogh, Vincent van Gogh to Wilhelmina, 1888.

In her desperation, God revealed himself and his plan for her child and the nations that would come from him.

Here is the twist: God normally reveals His name to man, that's the way it works. This is the one time in scripture where God allowed someone to name Him. Because God saw her when no one else did, Hagar called Him *El Roi—the God who sees.*

So she called the name of the Lord who spoke to her, "You are a God of seeing," for she said, "Truly here I have seen him who looks after me." (Gen. 16:13)

Hagar was stuck in The Gap. She made the Turn and lifted her Cry to God. When she felt most unseen, the Lord saw her, heard her, spoke to her, and showed her hope. When we see the One who sees us, everything changes. We can see a future and a way to move forward and bear fruit.

Waiting and Changing

Radical change is part of God's plan as He is walking us through our broken spaces. The goal is not merely a change in perspective or emotion. It is far deeper than that. It is a change of identity, of who we are, and of who we see God to be. It is ultimately a change in our relationship with God, the way we interact with Him.

The other great Reveal is that our Father lovingly shows us the idols that are wrapped around our hearts. In Psalm 42, the idols revealed are:

Fear of being abandoned
Fear of not measuring up
Fear of an unsure future
Fear of lack of control
Fear of lack of provision
Fear of anxiety
Fear of enemies

All of these are expressions of an orphan heart, of living like we have no Father to care for us. We can all relate to many of these fears. On our lament journey, we see the ways in which we have forsaken the Living Water and dug for ourselves broken cisterns that can never hold water (see Jer. 2:13). There is a realignment that blooms from the fresh revelation of God. And there is a holy waiting that begins as he works in us. The prophets tell us that in this waiting there is renewed strength (see Isa. 40:31).

Waiting on the Lord—entwining myself with Him, braiding my soul into Him—is a comfort. Anticipating His work in me is comforting because I don't know what I need. I don't even know what to pray for. So I wait on Him. This is not passive waiting but active listening. It is paying attention in the night, drinking in the *hesed* hues of God.

The crisp and clear revelation of God begins to change our hearts. And this transformation in the heart produces the transition from despair to hope. It happens in nearly every lamenting psalm. We are moving toward hope. He sees me; I see Him. He is at work in me. With every pang, He is making pieces for the mosaic. I can endure the process if I can trust the Artist.

Wisdom from the School of Sorrow

What are the best ways to help a grieving friend?

The best way to help a friend who is struggling with loss is simply to be present. Don't try to relate, don't ask many questions. Validate their emotions, but don't try to fix them.

Treat them the same way you always have. If they have lost a loved one and you knew that person, share positive memories of that person with them. It helps keep their memories alive and assures their loved ones will not be forgotten. Practical help is also important. Ask if they have any needs and show up to help.

Suggest some sort of grief support and maybe be willing to attend with them when they are ready. Pray for them daily, for the ministry of the Holy Spirit to meet their needs.

Quote:

I'll never forget so many kindnesses when my mom was on hospice, but in particular, my dear friend Kirsten just showed up at my doorstep from her house over an hour away (when she had three kids under age four at home, too), and put several freezer meals in my freezer, a bunch of paper plates and plastic silverware so we wouldn't have to worry about dishes, and came and sat with me at the nursing home for a while and just listened. I didn't ask her to, didn't tell her to, she just...showed up, and it meant so much. Our church friends also brought meals, and it just was an obvious representation of Christ being right there in the mess, disguising himself as a pan of lasagna and a plate of cookies. (Christina H.)

CHAPTER SIX

The Wait

Save me, O God!
For the waters have come up to my neck.
I sink in deep mire,
where there is no foothold;
I have come into deep waters,
and the flood sweeps over me.
I am weary with my crying out;
my throat is parched.
My eyes grow dim
with waiting for my God.
—Psalms 69:1–3

Sun sparkles dance off the rippling river as the path emerges from the wood and smooths out by the waterway. The long, slow climb begins. The ride on this part of the trail is serene but constantly rises many hundred feet to a towering view of the water and the deep green ridges beyond. Every long ride holds a point where determination must kick in. The pace becomes an enduring wait. But it is not passive—it is a very active wait. You just have to settle in and keep the pedals moving. It's the only way to get to where you're going.

The body of water I ride beside today was created by one of the nearly fifty dams the Tennessee Valley Authority manages on the major tributaries of the Tennessee River. This project altered everything in this valley in the twentieth century, and my ancestors were right in the middle of it.

The gentle flow of the water on this day is very different from the formidable floods that formed this valley. The uncertainty of these waters forced my family to wait anxiously year after year to discover their fate. Each spring the surrounding mountainsides funneled heavy rains into devastating floods, washing away the earth and sometimes the houses, barns, and livestock as well. Some years the floods were an inconvenience; other years they were catastrophic. My grandfather owned his land, and the family worked it hard, but every year was a lottery and their fortune was always a guess at best.

But far away in Washington, men they had never seen were deciding their future: a massive initiative that would reshape the better part of seven states. Their plans would devastate my family and bless it at the same time. My grandfather had to sell his family's land and evacuate the homestead they built with their own hands. With the government's help, they dug up and relocated their family graves and then moved two counties away while the community they raised their children in was buried at the bottom of a lake.

More than three thousand families would have to leave their homes forever. But the intentional flooding of thousands of acres would bring an end to the uncertainty. It took a planned flood to end the devastation of the annual floods. The loss was very real but so was the gain that altered their future. The water flow was regulated, and life became more stable. And something no one dreamed of came as well: electricity for everyone. My family endured the pain of change for the promise of a better future.

David has his own floods to contend with, though his are not weather related. Engulfed by enemies, deluged by danger, his troubles threaten to pull him down with immense force into a terrifying torrent. Psalm 69 is his cry for help. He has recognized his gap; he has turned to God and unleashed his anger and fears on Him. He has asked the questions of his heart. He is waiting for answers. And he is reminded, yet again, of God's heart:

> *Answer me, O LORD, for your [hesed] is good;*
> *according to your abundant mercy, turn to me.*
> —Psalm 69:16

Answer me. I know who you are. I know how you feel about me. I need you to turn to me and say something. My eyes grow dim from waiting for my God.

The World of Wait

In the language of lament, it seems the prophets and singers have a favorite word to describe their experience. It is a word you and I would likely not consider a favorite. The word is *wait*. But this kind of waiting is not what you might think; this kind leads to life and strength and hope. Here we have another irony of lament: waiting and thriving can coexist. Just because we don't perceive God's work doesn't mean he isn't working. And just because we feel like we are under repair doesn't mean our lives can't go forward.

Waiting is both the most frustrating and the most productive step in the lamenting process. The Hebrew word for *wait* holds a picture of *entwining* with another. Imagine the braids of a rope being wrapped around each other so you don't know where one ends and the other begins. Together they become one, new, stronger rope. Waiting on the Lord is entwining myself with Him, braiding my soul into Him, and finding strength in the union.

This kind of expectant watching is not a waste of time. It is a posture of dependence and expectation—an act of faith, just like turning and crying. But trusting is full of tension because we don't know what He is doing. We don't know the timeline. We don't know how He will resolve the matter or how He is working now in ways we are not able to see. Waiting is not doing nothing; it is trusting God's work and responding to Him.

To wait is to be God-oriented in your grief. To me, this is a great comfort because it is the opposite of the adage, God helps those who help themselves. In our grief, we come to the understanding that the God of *hesed* is helping us when we cannot help ourselves. We are choosing not to look to outward sources for what we need. And this, which feels like doing nothing, is filling us with great power, as Isaiah says:

But they who wait upon the LORD
shall renew their strength;
they shall mount up with wings like eagles;
they shall run and not be weary;
they shall walk and not faint.
—Isaiah 40:31

An eagle rises to great heights, but her power is not her own. Her body is designed to adapt to the flow of air, harness *its* power and soar on unseen currents with ease. The same thermal eddies of air that cause turbulence in airplanes (no one likes that) lift the eagle to heights.

When we entwine our lives with the Lord, we exchange our strength for His, and we rise to soar.

Like the eagles, we are designed to rely upon something unseen and greater than ourselves. It is not a weakness of the eagle that she depends on the power of the air. God has designed her to work with the turbulence and find in it her great strength. In the same way, in our waiting, we receive strength from the Lord of the storm. We orient ourselves to the currents of His grace and trust. He assures us with His own presence, and He speaks to our needs. We will not faint.

How God Works in Waiting

How does God spark hope and create a future where there appears to be none? How does He mold a new heart within us so we can see that future? We can get a clue by observing how He created all that we see around us. We have a firsthand account of that in the first verses of the Bible.

When God is at work it often looks like nothing is happening. In the creation account in Genesis 1, we see a shroud of darkness draping over nothingness. Everything is stuck; no movement. The earth was "wasteland and emptiness." Isn't this the way our world feels when we are stuck in our grief? But into this chaos comes two things that change everything: the presence of God and the voice of God.

At creation, the Spirit of God hovered over the face of the deep. This is the anchor in the waves of our grief journey. Remember that lament is a *holy space*. God is not somewhere far off watching you squirm in solitude. He is not distant and removed but right there with you, hovering over the face of your dark wasteland. He is not afraid of your chaos. He enters it willingly, boldly, and with personal interest.

On the journey of lament, we find that we are the very ones the Spirit chooses to hover over. He is right in the thick of our wounds and our cries, and like those first days of creation, He is recreating our hope and our future; he is restoring our souls. The Sovereign Lord is in control, and He is with me. I'm going to be all right.

With Day

On one of our wedding anniversaries, Melissa and I took a Caribbean cruise. When we arrived in the Bahamas, we paid a guide to take us around the island. I was surprised by the fact that there were hardly any people in the port, especially since it was a docking day for the cruise. When I asked the driver why this was so, he said it was a holiday. It was a Sunday, but I couldn't think of which holiday it might be, so I asked.

"Oh," he replied, "today is *With Day*."

"With Day? I'm not familiar with *With Day*."

"Well, you probably call it Pentecost, but since it is the day the Holy Spirit came to be with us, we call it *With Day*."

Something erupted inside me. Though I knew this truth and had taught it for years, the freshness somehow hit me at that moment. The nearness of the Spirit isn't just something that happens once a year. For followers of Jesus, *every day is With Day!*

> *"And I will ask the Father, and he will give you another Helper, to be with you forever… I will not leave you as orphans; I will come to you."* *(John 14:16,18)*

There is no greater comfort than knowing this truth. When I have felt my lowest during this grief journey, I have never been abandoned.

- I need the presence of one who loves me. *I have the Spirit inside* (John 14:16–18).
- I need a guide in my grief, for I haven't been this way before. *I have the Spirit as my Comforter* (John 14:26).
- I don't know how to pray. *I have the Spirit to intercede* (Rom. 8:26).

- I need the vision to see beyond my current pain. *I have the Spirit to show me things to come* (John 16:13).
- I need my wrong thoughts challenged. *I have the Spirit to convict and correct* (John 16:8).
- I need to be constrained sometimes. *I have the Spirit to hold me back* (Acts 16:6–7).
- I need the courage to go forward sometimes. *I have the Spirit to push me on* (Acts 16:9–10).

I am not an orphan, fending for myself. I am a beloved child, loved and led, covered and carried by the God of *hesed*. This truth is an anchor for me, but it doesn't stand alone. Not only is He with me but He speaks to me.

God is Not Silent

In creation, it was the voice of God that changed everything. Into the void of darkness, God spoke two simple, powerful words: "light, be." And this light is the basis for all of creation that follows. The comfort here is that God sets boundaries on darkness. Your dark times will not overcome you. He will speak light into your grief and pain. Weeping may endure for the night, but joy will come in the morning (Ps. 30:5).

Yet it often seems like he's silent. It seemed that way to the psalmists too. But the silence caused them to lean in, bend their ear and pay closer attention. And there it was, the light-spreading, life-giving voice of God. This is what happens in the waiting. When we don't know what we need, our very present Father will speak, and His voice changes everything.

Flawed but Faithful

I have never heard the audible voice of God. But sometimes there is an inner voice that shakes me so deeply it is louder than an audible voice. He speaks the vital things I need to know in the moment. Let me share a story with you.

Whenever I experience the periodic waves of grief over the loss of Melissa, my default memories often go to her last months. I am flooded with images of her suffering and those excruciating last weeks spent both at home and in the hospital.

The simplest of things that we all take for granted became very complicated. Sleeping was as much a task as a refuge for her because a comfortable position always seemed just out of her reach. Taking a simple shower became a great ordeal. Medication that helped in one area caused problems in another, necessitating more meds. How do we find the balance?

The pressing of tumors against her organs brought the need to shift in her chair and her bed. She put forth great effort to do simple things like moving from one room to another. She handled these difficulties with such grace, but I wanted with everything in me to be able to fix things, to come to her rescue and take away her pain. The inability to do this was the source of my own personal pain and is a core source of my grief.

But these memories do not represent the larger picture of our life together. And I need to be able to think correctly. I have found that it is important to confront the thoughts that I was not enough for Melissa, or that I could have loved her better. I think these thoughts are common to many who are grieving. The truth is no one is ever enough. I could not give Melissa all she needed because I did not have all she needed. My pain stems from the feeling that she was worth more than I was able to give her.

I needed to get God's perspective about this because I know that I tend to lean toward two opposite reactions. I can hide in my pride and have too high an estimation of myself. Or I can punish and pummel myself because all I see are my shortcomings.

On my sabbatical, I asked the honest question: *Father, can you tell me what kind of husband I was*? As I turned the volume down in my mind and turned the volume up in my heart, I believe I heard my very present Father speak three inaudible words that set me free: *flawed, but faithful*. These words were exactly what I needed to hear, and they were liberating because I know both things are true.

What We Long to Be

From the early days of our relationship decades ago, I wanted to be a blessing and a channel of healing for Melissa. I am painfully aware, and I deeply regret now, of the times when I didn't treat her as she deserved, when I stood back in my pride and fought for silly, petty things—when I was a source of pain, not healing. I was surely flawed.

But I was also faithful, by the grace of God. I was faithful to my wedding vows, and I tried to honor her before others. I took my responsibilities for her and the children seriously. I believe I provided a safe place for her to live and a safe place for her emotionally, at least most of the time. I made efforts to let her know she was special. While it is easy to focus on all that we could not do for our loved ones, it is crucial to remember that we did what we could. We showed them our love.

One of the kindest things Melissa ever said to me was a few weeks before she died. In the shadowed light of a quiet afternoon, when her pain had eased for just a while, she looked up from the journal she was writing in and said, "You've helped me know God better." What a gift those words are to me now. The accuser may scream my faults out to me, and I may agree with Him. But I know the truth. I heard it from Melissa and from my Father. In the end, I think "flawed, but faithful" is the best verdict we can hope for.

I came to realize that my PTSD default memories do not fairly represent our thirty-five years together. Those last months do not define our relationship. I have to remember the ways we experienced God, celebrated Him, and showed Him to others. The louder voice must be the years of laughing and worshiping and child-raising and trip-taking and date-dining and friend-visiting and anniversaries and graduations and all of life's joy. I mustn't let the loss steal the life and love we had.

God Does What We Cannot Do

When we realize God is at work in our grief and we lean in to trust and listen, He does what we cannot do. He stills our souls and anchors us in His love. He reassures us of his presence. He speaks things to us that give hope. He molds us into the image of his dear Son. He makes us what we need to be in order to step into the future and hope he has prepared for us.

At times we feel stuck and don't see any of what we would call "progress" in our grieving. But it is important to remember that *process is progress*. In the Wait is the strength. In those times we can surrender to the work of the Spirit and know He is active, healing, revealing, and giving us everything we need. This surrender is a beautiful kind of faith.

So, this kind of waiting is not passive; it is active and faith-filled. We are immersed in a gestation period. He births His Son deeply in and through us (see Gal. 4:19). This is a holy space. This is where God works.

When Melissa was pregnant with our twin girls, she went into pre-term labor at twenty-six weeks. Of course, birth at this stage would be high risk, especially for twins who have developed more slowly than a single child. It took a whole slew of doctors and nurses, a month in the hospital, a month at home on bedrest with meds and monitoring, and another week in the hospital to keep those babies in her womb. And when it was time, it took a heroic team of ob-gyn specialists, neonatologists, nurses, and anesthesiologists to deliver them.

Emily was head down and came first, but Allison was breech and had to be painstakingly positioned, manually maneuvered, and turned until she was head down by the two doctors who attended Melissa. They performed the in-utero inversion, and Melissa had to dilate again. It was two more hours of labor before Allison was born. In the end, Melissa was a hero, and the twins were born perfectly healthy. But they would not have been so at twenty-six weeks.

God is hovering over us, and as with Mary carrying Jesus, the Spirit is forming something inside of us. We can't rush the process. We have to wait. But we also must be carried by the hope that God is at work.

From of old no one has heard
or perceived by the ear,
no eye has seen a God besides you,
who acts for those who wait for him.
—Isaiah 64:4

Ask the Hard Questions

It is here in the waiting that strong faith rises up and the psalmists ask God boldly for what they need. Questions are an essential part of every biblical lament. They arise in us for a reason, and we should not shy away from them. There are no foolish questions. All of them are fair game, and God is not afraid of them. In my loss, I had many of them:

- How long will my life be defined by my loss?
- How do I live with heartbreak and hope at the same time?
- How do I honor Melissa's memory and still look to the future?
- How do I respond to people who don't know what to say to me?

- How do I continue to honor my family and friends? To love my children and grandchildren?
- What does my job and financial future look like?
- What does serving God look like now?
- Will I marry again?

I am inviting Jesus into these hard questions, these areas of pain and unsureness. Armed with a new perspective of who God is and a memory of what He has done—nestled in *hesed,* covered and carried by the kindness of my Father—I am finding that I can petition God boldly for what is lacking.

My needs are clear:
I need comfort in my searing pain.
I need perspective to see things from God's viewpoint.
I need to hear his voice step-by-step.
I need to learn what the new normal looks like.
I need the ability to see a future and faith to walk boldly into it.

It is in the waiting that we find answers to some of these questions and supply for our needs. The Wait is a crucial marker on the journey of lament, but we don't pass it only once. It is part of our intimate, ongoing relationship with the Father.

This Is a Journey

In my opinion, it is important to understand these steps of grieving are not merely something we check off the list, and then we are done. I wish it were that easy. But my grief is tied to my love for Melissa, so the only way to stop grieving her loss is to stop loving her. I'm sure that will never happen. Grieving may never end, but it does look different as time passes. And through the lamenting journey, we are changed so its effect on us is not the same.

Clarissa Moll, in her excellent book *Beyond the Darkness*, writes:

> *We move forward, not by finding closure, but by walking with grief, and thus in the footsteps of Jesus, who was acquainted with grief... We don't need to look for healing to find happiness. Closure is not necessary for flourishing.*[9]

Grief recovery is not a destination but a healing journey. Like the breath we breathe and the blood that pumps through our body with every beat of our heart, lament doesn't happen only once, but over and over. And each time it provides what we need to live and thrive. The furious flood waters that threaten to destroy us are reduced to gentle waves that change the shoreline over time.

Give yourself the grace you would give to others. It's okay to be where you are (this is good news since

9 Clarissa Moll, *Beyond the Darkness: A Gentle Guide for Living with Grief and Thriving after Loss* (Tyndale Momentum, 2022), 32–33.

you can't be anywhere else). Be patient with the process, but ask the questions. Sometimes as we ask the hard questions, they morph into more helpful questions through the guiding of the Spirit.

Why did Melissa suffer and die? I have asked the Father this question many times: in pain, in anger, in honest transparency, with a genuine desire to understand. I have not yet been given a specific answer, but I have been reassured of His kindness, presence, and sovereignty. My mind goes in speculative directions to try to wrench out an answer because I think, for some reason, I need an answer. But a wrong or presumed answer will not help me.

I believe there *is* an answer, rooted in the purposes and goodness of God. Melissa knows that answer now, as does my Father—but I do not. At my current state of the grief process, I'm not sure that *why* is such an important or fruitful question. I am sure I could get stuck here, becoming angry or bitter unless I am given a "reasonable" answer. That is certainly not profitable for me in the business I have before me: learning how to live in the new normal.

I can either stand back in pride, demanding an answer, or I can trust the God whose character I know. I know *what* happened, and I know *who* He is, but I may have to be content in not knowing *why*. I have told Him that I would like to know if He feels it is best to tell me. I have been honest with my pain and confusion. I have asked for help. Now I wait…and trust.

Waiting is another way we sit with our grief. The faith that rises up doesn't keep us from feeling the pain, but it sustains us in the pain and leads us toward hope. The One who has lost much more than any of us will faithfully comfort and guide us. Thank God we have a Man of Sorrows as a Savior. In your darkest moments, He is fighting for you, and He is changing you into one who can walk on into hope.

Wisdom from the School of Sorrow

What can I do when I feel alone or abandoned in my loss?

It's natural to feel our losses in many different areas of our lives when we are experiencing grief. It can feel like people are separating themselves from you or that you are alone on the journey.

It's important to make sure you are not isolating yourself from others. Identify friends you can call and talk to or cry it out with. Often people are willing to be present but don't know how to communicate that. They may think you want to be alone and not face the pressure of trying to socialize. Communicate your needs to those closest to you and don't let yourself grieve alone.

For some, it has been helpful to add to your life some things you may not have been able to do for a while. Find connections with others doing those same things. It can also help to look outward and serve others in some way.

Quote:

Loneliness, to me, is when I acutely feel the absence of connection to others and when you layer that with grief…wow. Immerse yourself in a project that serves another's needs and feeds your soul too. And with that comes new connections that help to make life bearable when you're having trouble moving one foot in front of the other. (Cheryl M.)

CHAPTER SEVEN

The Walk

For you have delivered my soul from death,
yes, my feet from falling,
that I may walk before God
in the light of life.
—Psalm 56:13

It's impossible to bike or hike anywhere without the memory of doing it with Melissa. As something we loved to do together, it is one of the countless triggers that may become less intense over time but never cease.

A hike or marriage—or even an illness and death—it's all about walking a journey together. A joy shared is twice the joy; a trial shared is half the trial. The mountains (literal and figurative ones) were a constant throughout our life together. Our first date was wading across the shallow but swiftly flowing river to picnic by a secluded waterfall, only to hurriedly take shelter under a blanket, sitting awkwardly on a massive river rock, surprised by a summer storm.

The night I proposed to her we drove into the mountains and to the edge of the national park. A steady, set-in rain had fallen for two days straight. The windshield wipers on my 1965 Mustang were beating out time in tempo with the throbbing of my heart. I had asked Melissa to dress formally, so she knew something important might happen that night. She was stunning in her black evening dress, and I wore my tuxedo (yes, I owned a tuxedo—I was a jazz musician, after all).

The restaurant where we dined had a glass atrium looking into the forest with rain falling sleepily overhead and a harpist (yes, the restaurant had hired a harpist) playing a Dan Fogelberg tune. When the waitress asked if this was a special occasion, I answered, "Every occasion is special when I'm with her." Pretty slick, I know.

We finished our meal and drove up the side of a ridge to an overlook, the rain relentless and my mind wondering how I would pull this off. But when we reached the overlook, the rain unexplainably stopped. It just stopped. We got out of the car, and a sight I'll never forget occurred. As we held hands and leaned against the hood, the clouds parted (like a movie moment, too good to be true) to reveal a full moon, shining silver and cresting over the opposing ridge line. Magical. There was just enough time for me to grab my guitar from the trunk, sing her a song I had written, ask her the question, and hear her response—and then the clouds closed, and the rains came again. It rained all the way back home... but the sun was shining in our souls. It was as if we were just actors in a marvelous production whose writer and director were our loving Father.

Learning to Walk

That walk to the waterfall on our first date and the walk down the aisle were only the first steps of our journey. Through the years we would periodically watch our wedding video. We laughed (cringed, actually) at the strange hairstyles, fashion, and color of the dresses. And those vows we had written ourselves—we were committing to some really lofty ideals. I remember watching the video of me speaking my wedding vows and thinking, *That boy has no idea what he is promising.*

I would come to learn that, as great and anticipated as the wedding and honeymoon are, after that comes the marriage. And the marriage is *very* daily. The marriage is waking up each morning and making decisions that are consistent with the promises we made at that altar. That's what it really means to walk together. Walking with God is the same.

When the Bible speaks of our relationship with God, it often refers to a walk. The walk is making decisions every day that are consistent with my commitment to God, made possible by his commitment to me. So the walk is a combination of entwining ourselves with God and pressing into those people he has placed in our lives. Even in our sorrow, the commitment continues—we walk on with God and with others.

One of our favorite bike rides was the loop around Cades Cove in the Great Smoky Mountains National Park. The Cove is a geographical wonder—a sprawling, fertile valley spread out amidst some of the highest mountains in the Appalachians. The first European settlers found the cove nestled among the ridges in the early 1800s. The irony of living in these mountains is that folks had to be rugged, independent types, determined to work hard to build a life. But also, survival on the frontier was impossible without the community.

These mountains, you see, are not proud peaks standing alone, they are ridges that fold in on one another and catch one another and lift one another. That's the way life happens around here. In the Bible, there are some laments that are sung alone to God and others that are sung in community. So we learn to walk on with God and with each other.

Walking on with God

Getting your bearings in the first months and years after a great loss can be difficult. The seemingly endless string of firsts are aches and epiphanies: the first Thanksgiving and Christmas, the first New Year and Valentine's Day, our wedding anniversary, and Melissa's birthday. And the questions that I never had to face before, for which I had no answers:

Do I continue to wear my wedding ring?

What do I do with her clothes and other possessions?

How do I cook for one person?

What things that characterized our life together need to stay the same, and what needs to change?

I have found it takes real courage to grieve. To get up, baptized in the pain of loss, feeling numb and unmotivated, and make the bed, make the breakfast, make the day—that is real bravery. But it doesn't feel like courage. It feels like inadequacy; like struggle; like trudging through mud up to your knees; like being asked to do something you are not equipped to do. And in this daily courage, there is a sweet surrendering to grief, like the sweetness when you surrender to love. There is a surrendering to the power that comes from somewhere else that is sustaining you now.

This is all part of living life in the threshold—the liminal space where I'm not what I was, but not yet what I will be. These pains of great loss are also opportunities to celebrate what we had together that many never get to experience. I can walk on with Melissa, continuing to remember and be thankful for who we were. The threshold can be a confusing place, but if we pay attention, we can feel the Bridegroom lift us over it and into a new and hopeful future.

Grief and loss are very real experiences, and they shake us to our bones. They alter us, but they do not define us. I am strengthened by the realization that my life is not defined by my loss but by my Lord. I am told in the scriptures that I am a child of my Father, chosen, adopted, accepted, redeemed, forgiven, given an eternal inheritance, sealed by his Spirit, and the doing of all this was my Father's good pleasure (see Eph. 1). Pressing into this truth and into the work that Christ has done to make these things possible has been the key to keeping me above water during the flood. Knowing God and His heart for me has made all the difference.

In another famous Psalm, David gives us a powerful insight into what happens in the dark waiting. The beloved Psalm 23 is the song of one who is nestled in the care of his Shepherd and Maker. It is also an admission that it's not all cheery and bright being a sheep. As inhabitants of earth, we go through difficult things, most of which we did not sign up for:

- Some are of our own making, bad choices we have made—these we need to learn from or repent for.
- Some are done to us—for these we must forgive and work to reconcile relationships, if possible.
- Some of them are just a natural part of living here. Going through them does not mean we are bad people or that we have done bad things—it simply means we are human beings living in a fallen world. Good things happen to all kinds of people; bad things happen to all kinds of people.

Like the Valley of Baca, we read about in Psalm 84, the shepherd psalm views life as a pilgrimage, and the journey takes us through the valley of weeping. In that valley, we find our Shepherd with us. This psalm speaks of three fearful things: death, evil, and enemies (constant themes in the lamenting Psalms). None of which we have to fear if the Lord is our Shepherd.

Shepherds oftentimes had to move their sheep from one field to another and sometimes that meant leading them through ravines to get to the next pasture. These were dangerous places, and without the shepherd, the sheep would get lost and would be easy targets for animals of prey. The slopes would have been steep and treacherous but the shepherds knew the way through.

It is in these times the sheep paid particularly close attention to the Shepherd. He didn't *drive* them, he *led* them, and they watched and followed him through the treacherous valley.

David is a master songwriter, and what comes next is a vital theological truth delivered in subtle, beautiful poetry. In that dark valley, and ever after, the pronouns in the psalm change from "he" to "you." David no longer speaks *about* God, but *to* Him, and from that point, his trust is unwavering. In the dark valleys of our lives, we find even greater intimacy with our Shepherd.

Once I had the opportunity to walk with shepherds on their annual trip up to the highland meadows in southern Poland. The trip was beautiful and exhausting, but the sweet, pastoral image that comes up in your mind when you think of sheep is not the entire picture. This was mud and dung, sweat and smell, constant care and vigilance over tricky terrain—and sheep that are completely clueless and dependent on their shepherd.

This particular trip was about ninety miles of difficult travel over a six-day journey. As we trudged through the hillsides, the experienced members of our group told me a story of what happened on this same journey just one year earlier. Along the way, several days into the journey, one young sheep was too weak to carry on and lay down in the grass apart from the other sheep. When one of our group attempted to pick it up, it became anxious and began to wrestle and wriggle, trying to loosen itself from his arms.

The man gently turned the sheep's face toward his own to make eye contact. He pulled the sheep to his breast so the heartbeat of the lamb could sense his own heartbeat. As their hearts began to beat together, the sheep calmed and could be carried and cared for. In the same way, when we are weary, it is looking into the eyes of our Great Shepherd and drawing close to feel His heartbeat that can calm and strengthen us.

Our walk with God in grief is much like the walk of Abraham:

> *By faith Abraham obeyed when he was called to go out to a place that he was to receive as an inheritance. And he went out, not knowing where he was going... for he was looking forward to the city that has foundations, whose designer and builder is God.*
> —Hebrews 11:8,10

The place we are going may be unknown to us, but it is designed and built by God. It is the fulfillment of His plan of blessing for our lives.

A year or so after Melissa's death, I was rummaging through a tote and found a journal I had written a few years after I came to faith in Christ and just before I met Melissa. I was amazed and amused to read my twenty-year-old self's writings. To my astonishment, I found myself in very much the same place as the young me. I didn't know what my future looked like; my source of income was unsettled; I didn't know if I would be married or remain single; matters of purity of mind and body were pressing. It can be dismaying to feel you are in the same place nearly forty years later.

But there is one thing I have now that my twenty-year-old self did not possess: decades of hindsight and life experience that have grounded me in a truth. When you place your future in God's hands, he is able to do with it far more than you can imagine. I have experienced my Father's faithfulness. So now, like David, walking through this valley, I can draw closer, know Him better, and trust Him with my future. And in the end, His "goodness and hesed follow me all the days of my life."

When these psalmists turn and cry out in pain to God; when they see more clearly this God of *hesed* and what he is doing inside them, something happens. They decide to take the next step in their walk with God.

I will give thanks to the Lord (Ps. 35:18).
I will confess my sin (Ps. 32:5).
I will trust you when I am afraid (Ps. 56:3).
I will remember your works (Ps. 77:11).

I will speak of your works (Ps. 145:5).
I will walk in my integrity (Ps. 26:11).

Even if their circumstances have not changed, they find themselves calmed, covered, and carried by kindness, and they renew their commitment to him. They walk on with him in practical ways.

Walking on with Myself

As we stay connected to God and allow his truths to change us, the way we view and talk to ourselves will change. We begin to find our identity and value, our significance and security in God. Our emotions and thoughts become more stable. But there are also physical and practical aspects of walking on with ourselves.

Your history, family ties, responsibilities, personality, and the nature of your loss are all unique to you. All that is happening to your mind, soul, and body can create a perfect gumbo of emotions, and your gumbo doesn't taste like anyone else's. Just like I have to adjust the seat and handlebars on the bike I use to fit my body, you have to understand your ride is unique to you. And just like I have to change gears on the trail when necessary, you have to adapt to your own speed of grieving and adjusting to your new normal.

Author Clarissa Moll reminds us, "One of the ways you can love yourself and keep loving your person is by taking care of yourself."[10] I can honor myself and help others around me by determining to take steps for my own mental, emotional, and physical health. My life circumstances have shifted and so have my mind and body. I have learned that I need to be active, practice gratitude, eat foods that fuel healing, sleep as best I can, and connect to other people.

Every meal or hike or sleep is a small step to moving forward without Melissa and with my children and grandchildren. It is important to prioritize my own well-being since I can't give to others if I am not well. These things will look different for me than they will for you, but it is proven that each small step will aid in bringing the healing our minds and bodies need after a grief trauma.

Simple things may need to be adjusted in your mindset. For example, losing a spouse to a terminal illness may cause you to never want to go to a doctor again or be in a hospital, but this isn't wise. Triggered memories may try to anchor you in the worst of times, but part of walking forward is remembering and celebrating the good times you had with your loved one. Learn to give yourself mental margin, space in your schedule, and rest

---

10 Clarissa Moll, *Beyond the Darkness: A Gentle Guide for Living with Grief and Thriving after Loss* (Tyndale Momentum, 2022), 69.

time for your body. Simplify, organize, and focus on the things that are essential.

The phenomenon known as "widow brain" is a real thing—I can tell you widower brain is too. After a loss, you may experience fog-like confusion or short-term memory loss. You may feel emotionally drained and unable to think a matter through to the end. This is simply one of the ways your brain copes with the added strain of grief. Much of this is normal and can be helped by exercise, nutrition, and sleep. I've learned to use memory aids and ask for help. I list things in order of what needs to be done and simply do the next thing on the list. There are many good books that deal with the mental, emotional, and physical aspects of grieving, some of which are listed in the endnotes throughout this book.

Mile Markers and How You Come to Them

It is not wise to compare our grief journey to others. But it is true that we come to many of the same mile markers on the grief journey. When I was on my sabbatical after Melissa's death, I covered a lot of miles. I used a GPS to guide me to some of the locations I was not as familiar with. One day as I looked down at it, I realized this is the very way my Father wants to guide me on my grief journey. Like a GPS, if I pan out to see the entire trip, I can't see the next turn. When I don't know my next step, I have to pan into the local view to get step-by-step instructions. Likewise, my Father will guide me, in a relationship, one turn at a time.

"I will instruct you and teach you in the way you should go; I will counsel you with my eye upon you" (Ps. 32:8).

"The steps of a man are established by the Lord, when he delights in his way" (Ps. 37:23).

"But the path of the righteous is like the light of dawn, which shines brighter and brighter until the full day" (Prov. 4:18).

There is a path of the righteous, but its awareness comes one step at a time. This is the way to greater intimacy and a stable soul.

When he asks, "What is your greatest need?" I answer, "You."

When I ask, "What's next? What do you want?", He answers, "You."

Common Mile Markers in Grieving

Zach and Maria were dear friends of ours for many years. One month before Melissa died, Maria lost Zach suddenly to a COVID-19 related illness. Though our marriages, our personalities, and our ways of processing grief are different, Maria and I have come to many of the same mile markers on our grief journey. They may be the same ones you come to—different routes, for our Shepherd tenderly guides us according to our needs—but similar truths we discover.

Our insights are from a faith perspective and from the specific angle of losing a spouse. Your loss may be different, but your mile markers may be similar.

I have come to the realization that:

- I am going to keep breathing and keep living without my person.
- It is my choice and responsibility to get out of bed each morning, make it up, put clothes on, and look to God to take each step through each day to do the next thing to survive, live, trust, and eventually thrive.
- Grief and loss profoundly affect every part of our being and will take time and effort to heal.
- I cannot hurry along the healing. But I can find ways to support my body, spirit, and soul during this exhausting process of grieving by practicing kind self-care.
- It is okay—and necessary for some—to seek medical, professional, and mental health care for support and healing through the grief process.

- Grieving is not going to go away. It is now a part of my life. Over time, it becomes less frequent and less intense. But it will still show up strongly at surprising times, triggered by surprising things.
- I need to find healthy ways to express and manage grief. (I cannot run away from it, for it will find me eventually and manifest in unhealthy ways).
- I need others to walk alongside me through this difficult journey. Isolating myself is only going to hurt me and make my grief journey even harder and lonelier.
- I will eventually come to a place of accepting that my person is gone and that my life will continue, as different and difficult as that may be right now.
- God did not cease to be good, or to be present, when my person died.
- Staying close to God is essential in order to grieve and move forward in a healthy way. Though it raises myriad questions and doubts—which God is not afraid of—it keeps me from falling into dangerous pits of self-medicating, isolation, self-pity, and despair.
- My core identity is in Christ. It is not tied to my loss and what is now missing from my life.
- There is hope that I can still have a meaningful, rich life without my person. Hope is a key to healing.

- My life still matters as long as I am on this earth. I have a call and purpose as an individual, even without my person.
- I can experience both grief and joy simultaneously. I can learn to exist and thrive with both.
- Suffering is a part of life on earth, and as believers, it is a key to conforming me into Christ's image. It puts me in places where I learn about God's incredible love and provision for me in ways that I could never experience when things are going well. There is wisdom that comes only through suffering.
- Because I am living through traumatic loss, others are now drawn to me and may share their own stories of sorrow. (Broken people are often safe people.)
- Widows (widowers) and orphans are fiercely loved and protected by God. He is showing Himself willing and able to lovingly, specifically provide and care for my needs.
- My heart is big enough to love others, even after this devastating loss. As I become more confident in God's love and care for me, the more willing I am to risk loving others.

Walking on with Others

Although many lamenting Psalms are written and sung from the viewpoint of an individual, there are also many that are communal. These hymns call an entire community to prayer, mourning, and repentance.

"Save us, O LORD our God, and gather us from among the nations, that we may give thanks to your holy name and glory in your praise" (Ps. 106:47).

"Let your steadfast love (hesed), O LORD, be upon us, even as we hope in you" (Ps. 33:22).

"Restore us, O God; let your face shine, that we may be saved!" (Ps. 80:3).

We can't always lament in isolation. While it is true there are some things others can't do for you, it is equally true that there are things you can't do without the help of those around you. This is true for us today as it was for our ancestors who settled this land before us.

The difficult winters, sickness, and troubles from wild animals meant that early settlers in Cades Cove supported each other as a means of survival. Clearing land, building houses and barns, milling corn, blacksmithing, carpentry, birthing children, providing sons and daughters to marry, and burying the dead. From the womb to the tomb, the community struggled, suffered, celebrated, and survived together.

It is important for us to open up to those God has put around us in order to survive grief. One practical way I have found to do that is to simply ask for help. Many people want to help but have no idea how they can. Often, they are very willing to invest time and talent to help. It is a small thing to them, but it may be huge to you.

Form Your Posse

Find the people around you who can help you do the things that are not easy for you right now. Here is a way to start:

- *Who is your relator?* This person is a safe place you can go and open your soul up to; they can listen and empathize and encourage.
- *Who is your doer?* This person sees a need or catches an idea and can make it happen. They have the focus and energy you may lack at the moment. They can organize your room or clean your gutters, mow your lawn, run your errands. They may be able to get more done in a day than you could in a week.
- *Who is your strategist?* This person sees the big picture, which may be hard for you right now. They can help with ideas and processes, finances and projects; they can see the future and a way for you to get there.

- *Who is your challenger?* This person will gently push you forward when you need it. They help with momentum and communication, and they can expand your social network to help get other things done. They may become your temporary social planner, helping you stay connected through supportive relationships.

You will need each of these members of your posse at different times, but they cannot help you unless you ask—so ask.

Draw boundaries. Honestly, there may be some people you need to remove from your life for the time being. They bring negativity and suck the life out of you. Proper social boundaries, even if temporary, are important when you are grieving.

Processing with your family is very important. I understand this is highly subject to your personal family situation, but families need each other during times of loss. If relationships are healthy, commit to communicating regularly with one another. Put a reminder on your phone to call and check on one another. Get together physically when possible and make sure to make the times supportive and remember the good times with a lost loved one. If your relationship with family is strained, at least try to do these things as much as possible. And let's not forget the most valuable balm for our families: prayer.

Don't avoid the sanctuary. In Psalm 73, David was completely perplexed by his circumstances and didn't get any answers until he went to the sanctuary. Don't forsake assembling with other believers. The role of the body of Christ in mourning is huge. No one can do this kind of trauma alone. I am forever grateful for my network of supportive friends, church, family, and healthcare professionals who have helped me in my grieving.

Finally, realize that you have something to offer others as well, even in your hard place. Oftentimes our healing process is sped up by our giving out to others in turn.

How to Help Someone Who Is Grieving

Most people are uncomfortable talking to someone who is grieving because they don't know what to say. It's difficult to know how to respond to a loved one who has experienced deep loss. People don't know what to do so sometimes they avoid you. Or they say something very inappropriate. Sometimes they are grieving the death of your loved one too, and it's difficult for them to be with you because it reminds them of their own grief. It can be understandably awkward. So, how do we help people in pain?

Here is what I can tell you: People in pain don't need answers. They need an ear. Your presence is the greatest gift. Your love is all they need. When the time comes that they ask you for your wisdom, then you can talk. But a general rule is the deeper the loss, the less you say and the more you listen and love (whatever love looks like in the situation).

Walking on with Our Loved One

In her moving and helpful TED talk on grief, Nora McInerny, speaking about the loss of her husband, Aaron, to cancer, reminds us that: "I've not moved on from Aaron, I've moved forward with him."[11]

This is an important insight. It is impossible to "move on," for that implies that the chapter in our life that included our loved one is over. The truth is, Melissa has shaped me and our children so much that we will carry her forward in a thousand ways. So the question for me is how will I live today in a way that will honor Melissa, love my kids, and serve my Lord Jesus? How do I honor Melissa's legacy?

One way our family has done this is by remembering her and not being afraid to talk about her in our

11 Nora McInerny, "We Don't 'Move on' from Grief. We Move forward with It," TED TALKS, April 2019, video, 15:05, https://www.ted.com/talks/nora_mcinerny_we_don_t_move_on_from_grief_we_move_forward_with_it.

gatherings. We also designed and built a memorial garden in our backyard that helps us remember Melissa. But one of the most significant ways we are honoring her legacy is The Melissa Movement.[12]

Our family loved the fact that Melissa had the heart to see other women mentored in parenting, marriage, and in the gospel. Our desire is to see that same heart multiplied to others, so we set up The Melissa Movement, a fund that promotes spiritual mothering in the body of Christ. Spiritual mothers are women who have a heart to befriend, teach, and mentor younger women in practical issues and in the gospel of Christ. This fund enables women who have a similar heart as Melissa to continue this vital discipline work, both locally and in the nations.

We are currently helping enable spiritual mothering in a local safe house that cares for teenagers who have been rescued from sex trafficking, in a remote Maasai village in Tanzania, and among young mothers in our local church. These efforts have helped us grieve by honoring Melissa's passion for younger women. She lives on in this ministry to others who were so important to her.

---

12 See www.markmedley.org

Walking into Hope

So walking has to do with connecting to people and to God. It has to do with making decisions every day that are consistent with our commitment to him, empowered by all he has done in his commitment to us.

David's lament in Psalm 56 expresses a beautiful and surprisingly intimate picture of God's heart toward us.

You have kept count of my tossings;
put my tears in your bottle.
Are they not in your book?
—Psalm 56:8

God has a bottle, and He has a book. Jesus assures us that there will be a day when every secret will be revealed. It will be known because the books will be opened. God not only deals righteously with the oppressor, but His heart breaks for the oppressed. He sees your tears, He counts them, and He will be faithful to comfort all who are suffering. So the conclusion of David's lament was:

For you have delivered my soul from death,
yes, my feet from falling,
that I may walk before God
in the light of life.
—Psalm 56:13

The way of lament ends at a place called hope.

Wisdom from the School of Sorrow

What do I do when well-meaning people say or do hurtful things?

It depends on what was said and your emotional state. In some cases, you just assume they had good intentions and let it roll off your back. Most people want to be helpful but may say hurtful things out of ignorance. You've got enough on you dealing with your loss, so if possible, let it go.

If you can't let it go, or if it's harmful to the degree that you or your family is being affected, go to the offender and tell them. They can't do better if they don't know better.

For example, "*Thank you for your care, but that is a hard thing for me to hear right now because I feel ______ when you say ______.*"

This way you acknowledge their intentions, advocate for yourself, and educate them on how to approach a grieving person. It's not easy to do, but some will be thankful because they honestly didn't realize it.

Quote:

I noticed that when I went through cancer, well-meaning folks thought it would be empathetic to share one of their relatives' cancer stories in tremendous detail. To say this was the opposite of what I needed would be an understatement.

Many don't know what to say or do for their friend going through grief, so they avoid and ignore them. I had two friends I saw weekly that had gone through cancer and the death of a parent and had been isolated by close friends. So they knew the greatest gift they could give was acting normal... like doing fun things and getting a workout from laughing so hard. Then when I needed to break down and cry, or just needed a sounding board, they listened. They told me, "If you want advice, ask us, other than that, we are going to listen, empathize, and give you normal." What a precious gift. (Lisa M.)

CHAPTER EIGHT

The Hope

Weeping may tarry for the night,
but joy comes with the morning.
—Psalm 30:5b

It rolls in like ocean waves over the creases and folds of the mountains. Because of this, the Native Cherokee considered this land a sacred place. They referred to the area as *Sha-Kon-O-Hey: land of the blue smoke*. Its ever-changing, mesmerizing mist is the reason these are called the Smoky Mountains.

This vapor-veil that wraps the ridges isn't such a mystery though. It is a fog that arises from millions of trees, bushes, and other plants that literally breathe out their silent sigh in the form of an organic compound. It carpets the ridges until only the highest peaks seem to float on its dreamy haze.

But on a terrifying Thanksgiving week in 2016, the smoke was not dreamy; it was a nightmare. Late one night, two teenage boys climbed one of the highest peaks and lit a match that, fueled by winds that whipped to one hundred mph, broke forth in a hellish-orange fury. The catastrophic fire burnt 17,000 acres in a matter of hours, killing fourteen people and destroying over 2,400 homes and businesses.

But from tragedy springs hope, for God has set a new life in motion deep within the DNA of the plants. If you traveled to these ridges just eighteen months after the fire, you would have seen the burnt and blistered landscape had become a sea of dense, deep green shoots of the Table Mountain pine tree rising one to two feet from the charred ground, stretching upward to the sun. This species has developed very thick, compact, and calloused cones that are literally glued shut with a strong resin. They hold their seeds for decades until intense heat from a fire allows them to be released and germinate. Without the fire, the species would die out.

Many ecosystems on our planet depend on periodic fire events to rejuvenate growth and ensure long-term survival. A controlled burn is any fire intentionally ignited to manage the land. These fires burn away underbrush and invasive plants and restore health in the ecosystem. They prepare the area for new growth and benefit the animals who live there. The hope of the future comes from the fire.

In these parts, they sometimes call controlled burning events *salting the earth with fire.* It is a term Jesus used (see Mark 9:49), and it refers to purification. It is curious that when complete destruction is described in history, both salt and fire are used. Cities are burned to the ground, and the land is sown with salt. Both salt and fire purify by burning, each in its own way. Salt and fire can be used to destroy, but in a controlled application, they can purify and preserve, heal, and enhance.

New life can come out of devastating circumstances. God is full of infinitely creative ways to enfold my trauma story into his redemptive story.

And I am sure of this, that he who began a good work in you will bring it to completion at the day of Jesus Christ (see Phil. 1:6).

Could it be God is restoring my health to me? That he is bringing forth new growth? That there is a bright future? If biblical lament teaches us anything, it's that the answer is yes.

In the book of Lamentations (the most obvious and pain-filled lament in the Bible), Jeremiah the weeping prophet walks us through the devastating reality of God's people. Jerusalem, the "joy of all the earth," had once been a great city but is now rotting in captivity, overtaken by enemies. Mothers and fathers, sons and daughters suffer bitterly in exile. They trade their treasures for a morsel of bread as infants cry in hunger in the streets. There is talk of cannibalism, of chewing gravel, and of groveling in ashes. There is no one to comfort her, only wasted skin and broken bones.

But from this desolation arises a lament song. And from the lament arises a prophetic promise of a bright future:

> *But this I call to mind,*
> *and therefore I have hope:*
> *The steadfast love of the Lord never ceases;*
> *his mercies* [heseds] *never come to an end;*
> *they are new every morning;*
> *great is your faithfulness.*
> "*The Lord is my portion,*" *says my soul,*
> "*therefore I will hope in him.*"
> —Lamentations 3:21–24

The way of lament ends at a place called hope. As I did my study of the lamenting Psalms, I made an unexpected discovery: laments often contain prophecy. This is because God often speaks his right-now word into the right-now situation the griever is experiencing. Fresh faith arises from the revelation of God's faithfulness. Fresh vision comes to us as we begin to see the "God who sees." Laments often turn prophetic as the person and purposes of God are revealed.

We often find lamenting songs in the middle of prophetic books of the Bible. This is because God is neither absent nor silent in our pain. Even more amazing, the prophecies we find in these laments are often Messianic because Jesus is revealed in lament. Jesus is there in the midst of our pain. A future and hope, the revelation of God's Son, and the release of his redeeming work—they are all there on the lament road.

None of this takes away the real anguish of our loss, but as we journey down the road of lament God shows us a pathway from our heartbreak to hope. Since Melissa's death, in many ways, I feel like Jacob, who wrestled with the angel and was forever marred—but whose name and destiny were changed. Because of my loss, I will always walk with a limp. But as I continue walking with God, He will change who I am for his good purposes. In the crucible, I've been given a gift—the holy *hesed* of God—and I will never be the same. Our lives will never be what they were when Melissa was alive, but my family and I will walk on, carried by the kindness of God, and we will find God's new future.

As sure as we can love, we can grieve. And as sure as we feel grief, we can feel hope begin to rise. While we are singing our lament song—turning, crying, seeing, waiting, walking—God is always working. For he feels the gap with us and turns toward us. He cries out for us and opens himself to us. He knows us intimately, and He asks the questions we need to hear. He walks with us. It is a dance, this lament, and he is the leader.

In Psalm 30 David—quite the dancer himself—recounts what he experienced when his midnight weeping was followed by morning joy. Once again, he cries out to God and his mourning breaks forth into dancing, with garments of gladness and a song that cannot be silenced.

> *Hear, O Lord, and be merciful to me!*
> *O Lord, be my helper!*
> *You have turned for me*
> *my mourning into dancing;*
> *you have loosed my sackcloth*
> *and clothed me with gladness*
> —Psalms 30:10–11

Many years ago there was a dance instructor who attended our church. As a service to married couples, she decided to give free ballroom dance lessons to any who were interested. Melissa thought it would be a great idea. I, on the other hand, knowing myself well, didn't think it was a smart thing to do. You see, I have lots of rhythm, and I feel the groove of music deep in my bones. But when I try to express that groove by moving my body, let's just say it gets lost in the translation. In short, I am no dancer. But I loved my wife, and to honor her, I went along. It'll be fun, right?

Our instructor patiently walked us through the simple box-step pattern along with a dozen other inexperienced couples. When she saw my timid and mechanical steps, she came up to us and tapped me on the shoulder.

"When a couple dances, someone has to lead—that's you, and someone has to follow—that's Melissa. Here, I'll show you. I'm going to dance your part, and you are going to dance Melissa's."

She assumed the stance and began to lead me in a waltz. I immediately understood her point. The leader maintains the rhythm, knows the figures of the dance, and decides how he is going to lead. He adjusts his leading to accommodate what is going on around them to ensure he and his partner do not collide with another couple. He knows what is going on, he knows what he wants to happen, and he leads the partner accordingly. The follower reads the signals and flows along with him.

I learned a lot that day about waltzing, about marriage, and about walking with God. And now I know that the lesson applies to walking the grief journey. Lament is a dance, and God is the leader. He who was and is and is to come has been with me and is with me now. I know he will lead me into the unknown future.

The Dance of Lament

There are many trails in these ancient woods that lead to mountaintops. One of my and Melissa's favorites was the Chimney Tops trail. It is not for the faint of heart and takes some real perseverance, as it gains over 1,400 feet in less than two miles. But at the top, the view into the horizon of those ridges is magnificent.

And it is always the horizon that we love to see, isn't it? We will always travel to where we can look to the horizon, even if we can't make it there. The horizon is what gives us vision and hope.

What is the fascination with the horizon? There is no denying we are drawn to it—perhaps we are hard-wired, or hope-wired, that way. But it is so far away, and we are here. Right here is where life happens. It is here where we are able to touch and know the Father, receive the comfort of the Spirit, more fully know the Son. What's wrong with where we are? We can be nowhere else. And the only way to grow into what we can be is to be loved right where we are—here, today. We have no choice but to live in the now, but we also need hope and a future to look toward.

If I could, I would have taken Melissa's cancer, her suffering, and her death. But that wasn't an option. Then again, had I been able to take it from her, she would be here dealing with this grief and brokenness, walking this road of lament. The cold reality is that the dreams we shared for the latter years of our lives together died with her. But the bright truth is that doesn't mean dreaming is dead.

This is important. Some dreams may have died, but dreaming isn't dead. We can still see a horizon of hope that is unveiled as we lament to God.

He is still, today in my point of pain, who he was before: kind, gracious, sovereign, with me, trustworthy. My calling and purpose, his plans for my life, were in effect long before I met Melissa. They are still in effect after her death. God still has dreams for me. And his dreams come true.

This is the *brutifulness* of lament:

Shattered dreams and dreaming can coexist.
Uncertainty and confidence can coexist.
Grief and goodness can coexist.
Who I was and whom
I am becoming can coexist.
A broken world and a faithful
Father can coexist.

Every pain of loss can push me into thanksgiving for the gift that was given and lead me to bless his name. Psalm 42, the psalm we started our journey of lament with, has a refrain, repeated over and over:

Why are you downcast, O my soul,
and why are you in turmoil within me?
Hope in God; for I shall again praise him,
my salvation and my God.
My soul is cast down within me.
—Psalms 42:5–6

The problem is not that we have no hope but that we put hope in the wrong things. Jobs come and go, bank accounts dwindle, pipes leak, even stars burn out, and yes, the bodies of our loved ones give out. But the scripture says that the man or woman who hopes in the Lord will not be put to shame. Hope does not come from a change of circumstance; hope springs from what you know to be true, despite your circumstances.

The more we walk in the Spirit, the freer we are to enjoy this life without fear of losing it. The more hope we put in this world, the more we fear losing the small and fleeting things to which our lives are chained. Our spirits know there is more to this life than this life. They can soar above the temporal because the eternal is their homeland. When we transfer our hope from things that will perish to things that are eternal, our hope will never die.

Blessed be the God and Father
of our Lord Jesus Christ!
According to his great mercy, he has caused us

to be born again to a living hope through the resurrection of Jesus Christ from the dead.
—1 Peter 1:3

This living hope comes from knowing the character of God and knowing that He is with us. It comes from the undeniable and invincible finished work of Jesus Christ. Yes, we grieve, but we grieve with hope (see 1 Thess. 4:13–14). This is the power of Christ in our present pain. Because of the work of Jesus, we have an unshakable, living hope that sustains and strengthens us. Our hope is in the good news of the gospel.

Wisdom from the School of Sorrow

After my loss, how do I find my "new normal"?

For many, the "new normal" comes in steps: getting over the initial shock, understanding that getting stuck in grief doesn't help anyone, and determining to live on as my loved one would have wanted.

Eventually, a sense of "normalcy" returns. But you have to accept that it is nothing like the "old normal." Feeling the pain in fresh ways doesn't mean you aren't progressing in your grief process—it means you still love your person.

Prayer, grief support groups, and encouraging relationships grease the process. Fulfilling my loved one's wishes and doing things that honor him/her can help as well. Be true to existing relationships and be open to new ones. Don't be afraid of deep discussions about what you are experiencing.

Quote:

I grieve my son's prodigal choices daily. Not a day goes by that it doesn't affect me. But the call of God on my life also lays claim. So I "box up" that grief, I metaphorically write on the box, "God, You know," and I try to leave that box alone. The Holy Spirit has taught me a healthy compartmentalization so that the painful parts of my life don't taint or color all the beautiful parts. I have other children and a husband and friends who need me as the whole version of me. (Sheila A.)

CHAPTER NINE

The Good News

My God, my God, why have you forsaken me?
Why are you so far from saving me, from the words of my groaning?
—Psalm 22:1

He was a classic pioneer preacher: fearless and fiery, faith-filled and frontier-wise, with calloused hands and a softened heart. The Reverend Samuel Doak side-wound through The Gap with the flood of Scots-Irish Presbyterians brought a Christian message that permanently affected the western colonies. They were the vanguard of the pioneer migration, and they combined the bravery of their forefathers Robert the Bruce and William Wallace with the faith of their spiritual fathers John Calvin and John Knox—whose prayers Mary, Queen of Scots had feared "more than all the armies of Europe."

Princeton-educated and full of the Spirit, Doak was a man of exceptional character who spawned congregations of believers, many of which first met under trees by rivers, often with guns in tow. Some of these churches are still meeting today (I attended one of them while on a retreat to write this book). Inspired to take Christian education to the settlers in the West, he loaded pack horses with books and walked more than five hundred miles back and forth across the mountains.

Soon hundreds of families were streaming through Cumberland Gap. Down the rolling ridges, across rivers and bogs, into the valley, and sometimes back up into the mountains they came, building churches, schools, and thriving communities. Through flood and fire, death and delight, these settlers entered this land of promise. They brought very little with them, but the one indispensable thing for most of them was firmly lodged in their hearts: their faith.

Often entire communities crossed the mountains to become the core group of new churches and towns in Tennessee. Later, revivals would spring from frontier camp meetings where many heard the good news and received hope and healing. It took a hardy stock to tame this wild land, but men like Samuel Doak came not merely to settle in the new territory. They came to bring the kingdom and culture of another world to bear on these lands.

With the coming of these rugged settlers came a message of the grace of God and the sovereignty of God—two truths that sustained them through difficult times. In the message of the gospel, they found strength for this life and hope for the next. Of course, not all of them were believers, but the presence of these Christ-followers considerably influenced the ethics of the new land. It was this good news that created the environment that caused their hopes to become reality. The hope that carried them through their challenging times is the same hope we have access to in our time.

Why Psalm 22?

If the end of lament is kindness and hope, why conclude the book with a psalm about being forsaken? The answer is found at the core of the gospel we believe as Christians.

David goes through every stage of lament in this psalm. He senses his gap and turns in anger and agony to his God—who he is sure has forsaken him. He unleashes his guttural cry day and night, laying out in detail his desperate situation. God reveals himself as holy, trustworthy, and ruler of all the earth. David recalls how God has rescued him in the past and waits for God's help in the present. He renews his commitment to walk with God in praise and tell others about him. The song ends with a hope that he will live and generations will see God's works.

The entire lament journey is laid out here. And the very personal desperation he describes is a stunning, graphic, and detailed Messianic prophecy pointing to the suffering of Jesus. If you read Psalm 22 and John 19 side-by-side, you see the gospel of Christ in vivid form—predicted hundreds of years before and played out in real time in the death of Jesus.

Surrounded by enemies who despise and mock him, an innocent man is wrongly numbered with sinners. His hands and feet are pierced and onlookers gamble for a piece of his clothing. He is betrayed by his own people and mistreated horribly at the hands of an oppressive political system. But the song ends in hope, with families of nations turning to God in worship and the blessings of God extending to generations yet unborn.

The Jesus story is the lament of the ages. Not in spite of suffering, but through it, God's blessings come to the earth. This is the message of the Cross. God has shown his great *hesed* to us through the *Baca* sacrifice of Jesus Christ. From the valley of his own weeping, there has arisen a spring of hope and eternal life.

A Lamenting Gospel

As followers of Jesus, the gospel we believe is good news that finds its source in the loving and grieving heart of God. It is the story of:

- A holy God who weeps over a relationship that was broken by rejection from the other side.
- A loving God who grieves because he wants you and me with Him.
- A Man of Sorrows, who weeps at the tomb of a friend; at the overlook of a city who rejects him; and in a garden where he sees the incalculable sacrifice that must be made.
- A Savior who suffers the pain of rejection to reconcile us to Himself.

Jesus is the embodiment of God's *hesed* kindness. This is a God who stoops down and sacrifices everything to heal us and bring us to himself. You and I should *run* to a God like this.

Theology Becomes Real

It is sometimes odd to hear those who have gone through terrible trauma say something like, "I wouldn't trade the experience for anything." That makes no sense to most of us—about as much sense as David's "besieged city." But I get it.

Am I saying that I am glad I went through my pain? No, that's not the same thing. The point is not that I enjoyed the experience but rather that what I learned in the School of Sorrow is priceless. Now I know—really know—that there is a solid foundation in the *hesed* of my Father. I am unshakeable in the knowledge that there is a presence and a kindness and a stability that is beautiful and transforming and hopeful. My theology has become real to me.

I did not want Melissa to die. I wanted thirty-five more years with her. All I wanted was to love one woman true and long until we were both old and our bodies were giving out, and we would care for and usher each other into the arms of our Savior. For me, it happened too soon.

But I understand what people mean when they say they wouldn't trade their experience for anything. The statement doesn't have anything to do with what they have lost. They are talking about what they have gained. As we walk the road of lament, our faith becomes a very sure source of hope. In reality, our painful event ushers us into a deeper experience of all that God has provided for us in Jesus.

Melissa died on Yom Kippur, the Jewish Day of Atonement. In spite of the crushing pain of my loss, there was something beautiful about the fact that she went home on that day. I came to realize that though she is no longer with us, the astounding truth is that she is currently—at this very moment—experiencing the fullness of the atonement that Jesus died to provide her.

She is at home with her Father, experiencing life the way it was meant to be, without the effects of sin. She knows no more rejection, only acceptance. The pains of growing up in a dysfunctional family are totally healed. She fully knows how much she is loved. She has a new body, and all sickness is banished. There is no shame, and there is no sorrow—she will never cry or be anxious again. She has all the answers to the questions I still hold in my heart. She woke up lavished with all the fullness of the inheritance Jesus died to give her. *Brutiful.*

The Good News of Jesus Christ changes me at the core, on the inside. It sparks hope within me and enables me to walk in that wholeness day by day. Through lament, through the process of seeing my Father and the work his Spirit has done in me, I believe these things more than ever. And because of these truths, I know that Melissa is more alive than any of us.

And I heard a voice from heaven saying, "Write this: Blessed are the dead who die in the Lord from now on." "Blessed indeed," says the Spirit, "that they may rest from their labors, for their deeds follow them!" (Rev. 14:13).

Nourished at the Table.

We commemorate the death of our Savior regularly at the Lord's Table. The lament of his suffering has birthed us into a new life in God. The Table holds nourishment for us and truths that help us see a new horizon of hope:

- God has promised to fix the brokenness; he sent Jesus to carry out a plan to end all suffering.
- Jesus is the Resurrection and the Life. Whoever believes in him, though he dies, yet shall he live.
- Jesus conquered death, and as believers, we will not only live forever, we will do so in a new heaven and earth.
- There will be an end to lament because there will be an end to brokenness. Jesus Christ will make all things new.

The gospel lives and grows and bears fruit in us as we wait and walk in hope. It is the very power of God to those of us who believe:

- Power to be forgiven.
- Power to be declared not guilty by God.
- Power to be reconciled and live in a relationship with God.
- Power to become children of God.
- Power to be transformed and be like Him.
- Power to live forever in a new heaven and earth.

Through Christ, we are delivered from the penalty of sin, for the debt has been paid. We are delivered from the power of sin, for we died with Him, and He has raised us up to be free from sin's grasp. We will be delivered from the presence and effect of sin in heaven, for he has promised us this. The table of our Lord's suffering has nourished all our needs.

What the gospel is doing inside me is a very practical work. It is changing and empowering me day by day, enabling me to see hope and a future, in spite of my loss. As I move forward, I have found an important question that has helped me get my bearings. I think it might be helpful for you to ponder this question as well, though your answers may be different than mine.

How will I choose to live on with this grief?

- **I choose to live gratefully,** thankful for what I was given in Melissa, for my children and grandchildren, for relationships, and for provision far beyond my needs.
- **I choose to live in kindness**, carrying on the spirit of Melissa who always saw people, had time for them, and valued them enough to gift them with kind words and actions.
- **I choose to live generously**, to open my heart, my schedule, my bank account, and my possessions—to

pour out to others what my Father has poured into me.

- **I choose to live with purpose**, to finish strong, to be a father to my children, a papa to my grandchildren, and a builder in God's kingdom; to share wisdom and love with those my Father connects me within the nations; to communicate, in every way I can, the wonder of God's Word and kindness.
- **I choose to steward my brokenness.** To allow my pain to press me into Jesus and into thankfulness for what he has given me. To embrace my weakness and allow God to release his power through me to help others.

Long ago I gave all I am to God. Convinced He could do better with my life than I had done up to that point, I told him He is welcome to do with me what He wants. My point of surrender was an act of faith, for I had no idea what course my life would take in his hands. His goodness to me has been beyond my wildest dreams, and his greatest earthly kindness to me was Melissa. Loving her and being loved by her; the life we built together; the children God blessed our union with—these are more than I could have imagined.

But the pain of losing her is also more than I could have imagined. Somehow, it doesn't occur to us when we fall in love that one of us will die first and the other will take the blow. There is no other way. But I am still in his hands. All I am is His, and the biggest part of who I am presently is this pain. So, I find this incomprehensible grace of God working in me, causing me to say, "You can use my pain. I yield it to you. I will write the book. I will travel and spread the hope you have shown to me to others who are hurting. I will make myself available for radical kindness—the kind you have shown to me... the kind that takes our breath away." That sounds like something Melissa would do.

A Final Song

When I first met Melissa, we began leading worship together. She had a gorgeous voice (she will always be my favorite singer) and being the backup band for her was a privilege. Before we were dating, we sang a song together at church. I didn't know it would be the first of thousands we would sing together through the years.

Pedaling the bike that day along the river, through the valley and over that ridge, that very song came to me. During the turns and cries and the enduring, active wait—that day when God revealed Himself afresh to me—I recalled that first song we did together. I remembered it because it was an arrangement of Psalm 84, the valley of weeping song. The chorus of the song rings through my mind often:

You, O Lord, are a sun and a shield
You show us favor and honor
No good thing will you withhold
from him who walks with you
Almighty God...blessed is
the man who trusts in you.[13]

At the very beginning of our relationship and all the way to the end, this song rang true. God blessed us with life; He protected us and gave us his favor. It was the honor of my life to know and love Melissa. Solomon says, "He who finds a wife finds a good thing and obtains favor from the Lord" (Prov. 18:22). Melissa was my good thing.

Throughout the years when we were in congregational worship settings, at some point during the worship service, I would reach over and grab Melissa's hand, and we would sing together as one. They were always tender moments. This is what we had vowed our marriage would be. God had made us one and we would worship him as one.

In the last months of Melissa's life, we would lie together at bedtime and listen to worship songs. Sleep didn't come easy for her, and when it did, it was interrupted by pain or various reactions of her body

13 "Blessed Is the Man," Israel's Hope, track 5 on *Introducing Israel's Hope*, Omega Recording Studios, 1987.

to the medicine. We lay holding hands, singing of the goodness of God, as his *hesed* ministered to us even in our brokenness.

More than most things, I miss holding that hand in worship. But my lonely worship experience is informed by my faith. We are still worshiping together, just in different places: me, by faith through a dark glass...but she is worshiping face-to-face. Oh my, what she is seeing. My heart is happy that she is happy and whole. She deserves it more than anyone I know.

In our mountains, in our valleys, we have to remind ourselves of the beautiful provision God has given us in the gospel. Remind ourselves that the way of lament ends at a place called hope and that we will always be covered and carried by the kindness of God.

> *Return, O my soul, to your rest;*
> *for the Lord has dealt bountifully with you.*
> *For you have delivered my soul from death,*
> *My eyes from tears,*
> *My feet from stumbling;*
> *I will walk before the Lord*
> *in the land of the living.*
> —Psalms 116:7–9

[illegible] the [illegible] nothing [illegible] [illegible] friend [illegible] our [illegible]

N[illegible] I [illegible] [illegible] still [illegible] [illegible] different [illegible] (Mr [illegible] Mr [illegible] [illegible]

In our [illegible] kindness of God.

[illegible]

ACKNOWLEDGMENTS

I am indebted to many who have walked with me on this journey. Words cannot express my love and gratitude for my children—Katie, Emily, Ally, and Zac—along with their spouses and my extraordinary grandchildren. Walking through this grief together with you has made it bearable, even beautiful. The love and closeness we share is a great strength in my life. Your mom would be so proud of you.

This book could not have been written without the support of many friends, including the loving care of the pastoral team at Trinity Community Church in Knoxville. I am thankful for faithful friends, like Neil Silverberg, Mateusz Otremba, and Maria Richardson, for walking with me through this Valley of Baca and contributing to this project. Finally, thank you for the input and support of the team and fellow authors at hope*books who taught me that great books are written in community. All glory to God through our Lord Jesus Christ.

FOR FURTHER READING

Chapter 1

The following are references to helpful books that deal with the physical, psychological, and practical issues of grief:

1. Card, Michael. *A Sacred Sorrow: Reaching Out to God in the Lost Language of Lament*. (NavPress, 2005).

2. Crabb, Larry. *Shattered Dreams: God's Unexpected Path to Joy*. (Waterbrook Press, 2010).

3. Goll, James W. *Tell Your Heart to Sing Again*. (Broadstreet Publishing Group, 2020).

4. Hodges, Samuel J., Kathy Leonard. *Grieving with Hope: Finding Comfort as You Journey through Loss*. (Baker Books, 2011).

5. Keller, Timothy. *On Death*. (Penguin Books, 2020).

6. Lewis, C.S. *A Grief Observed*. (HarperCollins, 1961).

7. Moll, Clarissa. *Beyond the Darkness: A Gentle Guide for Living with Grief and Thriving after Loss.* (Tyndall Momentum, 2022).

8. Vroegop, Mark. *Dark Clouds, Deep Mercy, Discovering the Grace of Lament.* (Wheaton: Crossway, 2019).

9. Wright, H. Norman. *Experiencing Grief.* (B&H Books, 2004).

Made in United States
Troutdale, OR
03/03/2024